INUIT, WHALING, AND SUSTAINABILITY

Contemporary Native American Communities:
Stepping Stones to the Seventh Generation

Native American communities and people have survived through the twentieth century and are poised to embark on the twenty-first century. The survival and continuity of Native American cultures and communities has been a varied and complex path. Hundreds of communities continue to preserve many features of the religion, government, kinship organization, values, art, ceremony, and belief systems, and maintain political relations with the United States. The series is intended to fill an existing void in the literature on Native American contemporary world experiences. While providing a historical background, the series will focus on an interpretation of contemporary life and cultures, interpreted in their broadest contexts. The series will draw from the disciplines of Native American Studies, History, Sociology, Political Science, Religion, and Social Work, and solicit treatments of treaty interpretation, sovereign rights, incorporation into global and national economic, political, and cultural relations, land rights, subsistence rights, health and medicine, cultural preservation, contemporary spirituality, multiple genders, policy, and other issues that confront tribal communities and affect their possibilities for survival. New and culturally creative possibilities have emerged in film, theater, literature, dance, art, and other fields as a result and reflection of the challenges that have confronted Native American communities over the past centuries and will again in the coming century. We believe it is very important to examine contemporary Native American life from the point of view of Native concerns and values. Manuscripts that examine any significant aspect of Native American contemporary life and future trends are welcome.

Series editors' royalties will be donated to The UCLA Foundation/Yellowthunder Scholarship Fund.

Series Editors

Troy Johnson
American Indian Studies and History
California State University, Long Beach
Long Beach, CA 90840
trj@csulb.edu

Duane Champagne
American Indian Studies Center
3220 Campbell Hall
Box 951548
UCLA
Los Angeles, CA 90095-1548
champagn@ucla.edu

Editorial Board

INUIT, WHALING, AND SUSTAINABILITY

Milton M. R. Freeman
Lyudmila Bogoslovskaya
Richard A. Caulfield
Ingmar Egede
Igor I. Krupnik
Marc G. Stevenson

ALTAMIRA
PRESS

A Division of Sage Publications, Inc.
Walnut Creek • London • New Delhi

For information address:

AltaMira Press
A Division of Sage Publications, Inc.
1630 North Main Street, Suite 367
Walnut Creek, CA 94596
explore@altamira.sagepub.com
http://www.altamirapress.com

SAGE Publications Ltd.
6 Bonhill Street
London EC2A 4PU
United Kingdom

SAGE Publications India Pvt. Ltd.
M-32 Market
Greater Kailash 1
New Delhi 110 048
India

PRINTED IN THE UNITED STATES OF AMERICA

Library of Congress Cataloging-in-Publication Data

Inuit, whaling, and sustainability / Milton M. R. Freeman . . . [et al.].
    p. cm.
    Includes bibliographical references and index.
    ISBN 0-7619-9062-3 (cloth : acid-free paper)
    ISBN 0-7619-9063-1 (pbk. : acid-free paper)
    1. Inuit--Fishing. 2. Inuit--Social conditions. 3. Whaling--Government policy. 4. Whaling--Law and legislation. 5. Sustainable fisheries. 6. Sustainable development. I. Freeman, Milton M. R., 1934–
    E99.E7 I564 1998
    338.3'7295--ddc21   98-25451
                                                 CIP

99 00 01 02 03 04 7 6 5 4 3 2 1

Interior Design and Production by Rachel Fudge
Editorial Management by Jennifer R. Collier
Cover Design by Jennifer R. Collier

Table of Contents

Illustrations

Foreword

It is generally acknowledged that Inuit, living in a harsh and demanding environment, have over the centuries experienced and coped with many difficulties in order to survive. Today, thanks to modern conditions, life is much easier for most of us than it was for our ancestors. But modern times also bring their own particular challenges, and one of the most complex and difficult issues we face today concerns whaling.

Whaling has always presented a challenge, particularly when the whale being hunted was one of the larger species—say a bowhead, a gray whale, or a humpback. The challenge that whaling represents for us today is of quite a different kind, for it is not only the age-old one between hunter and prey, or between hunter and bad weather or the ice. The difficulty today is a more threatening conflict—it is a cultural conflict, one between different sets of values, between different philosophies and ways of understanding and appreciating nature and its wondrous creatures. It is the conflict between, on the one hand, a hunting people living for the most part in small coastal hamlets and towns in the Arctic, and, on the other hand, urban peoples living outside of the Arctic who, for a variety of reasons, now believe that whales should not be killed for food. However, despite our need to eat whales and other animals we hunt, we also share city dwellers' fascination and respect for these magnificent animals, and we will continue to work cooperatively with people living elsewhere to protect the health of the ocean ecosystem and the sustainability of whale populations.

However, in the Arctic, a land where agriculture cannot be practiced, hunting has always been our means of survival. As hunters, our people developed various social, cultural, and economic institutions and an associated system of belief, that have allowed us to appreciate the Arctic as a good place to live. We still believe that to be true, and today, many of us remain hunters. Indeed, the realities of the Arctic, even today, require that many among us continue to kill the animals we need in order to maintain our health, our communities, and our identity as Inuit. Food from the seas, the rivers, and the tundra is the desired and customary food of our elders and our children alike.

Like many peoples with distinctive languages and traditions of which we are proud, we wish to insure that our distinctive culture survives, and that it provides our children and grandchildren with a secure foundation enabling them to adapt to the world they will live in. For that reason, Inuit are willing to establish a dialogue with those who, for whatever reason, weaken our culture and our security through attacks upon our use of the animals that provide us with the necessities of life.

The Inuit Circumpolar Conference (ICC) has engaged in a study, the results of which are included in this book, whose purpose is to help promote such a constructive dialogue. In the following pages, the reader will find the well-considered views of Inuit living in Alaska, Canada, Siberia, and Greenland. Those who have contributed to this book include Inuit youth in the schools, hunters, and other men and women in the communities—some of whom are leaders, others of whom are not—and our respected elders. I am grateful to all those who took the time to participate, for their words are representative of Inuit everywhere, and they are sincere. For some participants, engaging in this dialogue doubtless caused anguish and pain, as they recall the consequences to their families and communities of others' misunderstanding and attacks.

We, the Inuit, seek to overcome the problems we face through an open dialogue based upon an honest examination of the facts, for we truly believe that such a dialogue will contribute to better understanding and coexistence. Despite globalisation, we believe that different and distinctive cultures and societies will long persist, and each in their own way will help make the world a more interesting, more secure, and richer place in which to live.

I wish to personally thank each of the authors who combined their knowledge and understanding of the Arctic and Inuit culture in order to place the words of the many Inuit contributors to the study into a coherent narrative. Mr. Ingmar Egede, a former Vice President of ICC, has represented the Inuit whaling position at many international meetings. Intimately familiar with the whaling issues in Greenland and abroad, his initiative and wisdom have been critical to this study from its inception to its conclusion. Dr. Richard Caulfield, from the University of Alaska, Fairbanks, has worked in the smaller hunting communities of West Greenland, and has taught at the University of Greenland, as well as having worked for many years in Inuit communities in Alaska. Dr. Igor Krupnik, at the Smithsonian Institution in Washington, D.C., has experience working in the whaling communities of Chukotka, as has Dr. Lyudmila Bogoslovskaya of the Russian Academy of Sciences in Moscow, who for many years has worked on joint research projects with Chukotkan marine-mammal hunters. Dr. Marc Stevenson has worked throughout the Canadian Arctic on such important issues as contaminants in local foods and current Inuit wildlife, whaling, and whale conservation programmes. Dr. Milton Freeman, who together with Dr. Stevenson is at the Canadian Circumpolar Institute in Edmonton, Alberta, coordinated the study and the final report. As with his colleagues, Dr. Freeman has worked for many years in the Arctic on whaling issues and on matters more generally related to Inuit subsistence and resource use. The ICC is grateful to the work of these researchers, and all the others who contributed to this study and whose names appear elsewhere in the book.

Aqqaluk Lynge
President, ICC

Preface

At the present time, new concepts and values are coming into Inuit life with the speed and power of driving snow in an Arctic blizzard. They change our minds and our livelihood; they enrich us, and they threaten us, but they do not change the Arctic where we live.

This book is about whaling. Apart from describing which whales are taken where, how, and by whom, it tells about the importance of the belugas, the narwhals, the grays, the bowheads, the minkes, and the fin whales. It allows people from Chukotka, Alaska, Canada, and Greenland to express themselves about hunting, about their food, about their culture, and about the inter-dependencies that structure our societies. They tell about the joy, the daring, and the pride associated with the hunt, and they also tell about the fear, the anger, and the helplessness they often feel towards the long-lasting and mis-guided actions of the International Whaling Commission (IWC).

Inuit, Whaling, and Sustainability does not deal only with these issues. It also tells about international laws, covenants, conventions, and strategies where relevant legal and human rights are described and defined, in an effort to show that the policy and actions of IWC are not in accordance with these international norms. In fact, the IWC is contradicting its own Convention—which instructs it to provide for the proper conservation of whale stocks and thus make possible the orderly development of the whaling industry. At some point in time, the IWC will have to revise its policies or its Convention in order to return international whaling policy to the path of reason and lawfulness.

The title of the book reflects the relationships among Inuit, their culture, and one of the modern world's relatively recent priorities—namely, the sustain-able use of living resources. Anyone who has observed a whale hunt will have seen how little disturbance is caused by the take of a large whale, or a number of small whales. Although the actual school of whales is momentarily disturbed, nevertheless they come back again, day after day, year after year. This we see as an illustration of the fact that we live as an integral part of nature. Because the marine mammals are the dominant source of food for coastal Inuit, sustainabil-ity has always been an important part of our culture. This is still reflected in the hunt, and in the hunting regulations maintained by the Inuit.

We are aware that politicians, who write the instructions to their repre-sentatives at the IWC, are under pressure from their constituents to protect and conserve whale stocks. We also know that this pressure comes from urban peo-ple, to whom nature is a dream, an ideal, and, in the vast majority of cases, have never had the opportunity to build up a realistic and profound relationship with nature.

We are for conservation of whale stocks; we respect our game, but we are against the simplistic notion expressed in slogans like "Save the Whale!".

That many whale stocks are healthy, and that people in the Arctic and in other coastal communities elsewhere continue to depend on a relatively small number of whales being taken, are often disturbing facts to whale protectionists and the public in general. When the public also learns that sustainability is a kind of second nature to the whalers of the North, they are often ready to soften their demands for an anti-whaling policy.

We want our people and our culture to survive on the basis of our traditions and on what the modern world can offer. We—maybe naively—believe that relevant information and knowledge can change people's attitudes toward our whaling traditions.

For many years, we have been adjusting to the modern world to which we belong. Now we think it is time that people in the Western world not only listen to us, but also learn from us, and consider adjusting their views toward our whaling practices. This book is our contribution to the process.

Ingmar Egede
Nuuk

Acknowledgments

A great many people have contributed to this book, and we would like to acknowledge their cooperation and assistance. To the many students and their teachers in schools in the eastern Canadian Arctic who undertook social studies projects on the topic of whaling, an especial "thank you!"; excerpts from their work are used liberally throughout this book.

Others, in four national capitals, also provided assistance in various ways. In Copenhagen, Einar Lemche; in Nuuk, Amalie Jessen, Hon. Paaviaaraq Heilmann, Hansi Kreutzmann, and Anton Siegstad; in Ottawa, Frank Andersen, Terry Fenge, Dan Goodman, Morley Hanson and students (from throughout Nunavut) attending Nunavut Sivuniksavut, Hon. Ron A. Irwin, Rosemarie Kuptana, Hon. André Ouellet, Chester Reimer, Mary Sillett, Ambassador Mary Simon, and Brian Wong; and in Washington, D.C., Douglas K. Hall and Stephen S. Boynton.

Many others have contributed in different ways to the work undertaken: the late Jay Akpalialuk; Simionie Akpalialuk; Johnny Mike; the members of the Pangnirtung Hunters and Trappers Organization; David Poiessie (all of Pangnirtung); David Kritterdlik and members of the Hunters and Trappers Organization of Whale Cove; Michael Kusugak (Rankin Inlet); Sam Emiktowt and members of the Hunters and Trappers Organization of Coral Harbour; Norman Snow, Duane Smith, and members of the Hunters and Trappers Committee of Inuvik; John MacDonald (Igloolik); Joe Enook, Josie Kusugak, Martha Toka, and Glen Williams (Iqaluit); Barbara Tagoona Beveridge (Repulse Bay); Russel Barsh (Lethbridge); Caleb Pungowiyi (Nome); Henry Huntington (Anchorage); Petr Aleinikov (Moscow); Don Dowler (Kelowna, B.C.); Gail Mathew (Edmonton); Jacob Adams, Thomas Albert, Maggie Ahmaogak, Arnold Brower, Jr., Charles Brower, Jr., Marie Adams Carroll, Edward Itta, Jeslie Kaleak, Sr., Burton Rexford, and Delbert Rexford (Barrow); Ussarqak Qujaukitsoq (Qaanaaq); Alexander Omrypkir and Tatyana Achirgina (Anadyr); Gennadyi Gygolnaut (Enmelen); Aleksei Agranaut, Vladimir Eineucheivun, Yurii Tototto, and Yakov Vukutagin (Inchoun); Sergei Penetegin and Lyubov Piskunova (Lorino); Seigei Rentin and Yurii Yatta (New Chaplino); Andrei Ankalin, Nikolai Gal'gaugye, Timofei Panangye, and Petr Typkhkak (Sireniki); Kim Akikak, Oleg Apkan, Vadim Ayautkak, Igor Leita, and Vyacheslav Kevkun (Uel'kak); and Konstantin Kymychgen (Yanrakynnot).

We gratefully acknowledge the use of photographs provided by the following: Dennis Alunik and Tusaayaksat (Inuvik; Figs. 7, 20), S. Bogoslavskii

(Moscow; Figure 21), Richard Caulfield (Fairbanks; Figs. 11, 24), Milton Freeman (Edmonton; Figs. 1, 2, 5, 8, 13, 15, 26, 31), Klaus Georg Hansen (Nuuk; Figs. 23, 32), Henry Huntington (Anchorage; Figs. 4, 12, 17, 18, 25, 30), Nikolai Konyukhov (Moscow; Figure 27), John Rasmussen (Narsaq; Figs. 22, 28), Rick Riewe (Winnipeg; Figs. 3, 6, 10, 16, 29), the Public Archives of Canada (Figure 19), and Hudson's Bay Company Archives (Figs. 9, 14).

Finally, we acknowledge the generous financial support obtained from the Department of Fisheries, Hunting and Agriculture, Greenland Home Rule Government; Department of Indian and Northern Affairs Canada; ISI (Indigenous Survival International); KNAPK (Kalaallit Nunaanni Aalisartut Piniartullu Kattuffiat); NAMMCO Fund of the North Atlantic Marine Mammal Commission; and Nature and People in the North.

Finally, the helpful advice and encouragement provided by Jennifer Collier of AltaMira Press, and the constructive suggestions of those who reviewed the manuscript for the publisher, are sincerely appreciated.

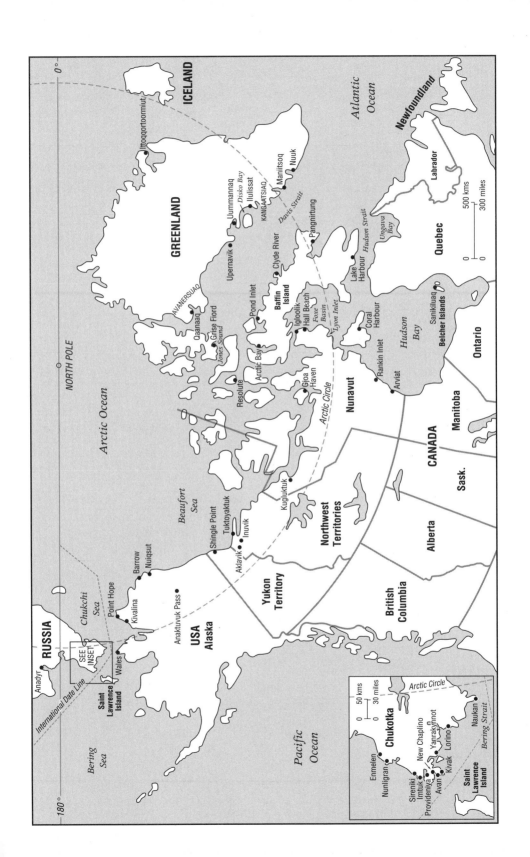

A Book on Inuit Whaling?

There are many wonderful animals, but whales are best of all. As they pass by your skin boat, great and quiet, you immediately come to understand your place on the Earth, and you become warm inside. . . . It is very interesting to look at whales, but most importantly, it is useful and necessary in order to become a full-fledged person—a hunter.

Nikolai Gal'gaugye, Sireniki, 1994

The reason I exist today as an Inuk is because of my ancestors that really tried and survived on wildlife [and] whales. . . . When I go whale hunting . . . there's a lot of things that go through my mind, not about the world today, but about the world where we were before, where my ancestors were coming from. Yeah, you can almost hear echoes [from the past] when you are whale hunting.

Johnny Mike, Pangnirtung, March 1995

So varied and profound are the bonds linking Inuit to the animals that supplied their means of survival for centuries, that it is not surprising that significant aspects of this relationship continue to exist today.

Although construction of dwellings no longer requires using the skins or bones of animals, such locally obtained materials continue to be used for essential footwear, winter clothing, boat coverings, and dozens of other uses throughout the Inuit homeland. However, it is especially in relation to meeting daily nutritional needs—as well as important social, economic, cultural, and emotional needs—that animals remain indispensable to Inuit everywhere.

This book describes and explains the nature of this continuing relationship by focusing on one prominent part of the human–animal resource complex in the Arctic, namely, that of Inuit and whales. Using, to the greatest extent possible, the words of Inuit who have commented on this particular relationship, the contents of this book emphasize the importance of whales and whaling to Inuit communities.

In the Arctic, where whales provide, in such abundance, so much that is necessary and beneficial for human well-being, Inuit continue to look to the whale for their physical and cultural sustenance, as their forebears have for millennia. This book illustrates the importance of the human–whale relationship among the Inuit as it existed in the distant and more immediate past, as it exists at the present time, and—as far as anyone can imagine—as it might exist in the future.

Although the future cannot be accurately predicted, it can nevertheless be imagined. In the modern world, small hunting societies in general and Inuit hunters in particular have reason to be concerned about their futures, and these concerns will be raised in this book. Reassuring answers to these concerns are beyond our reach, but raising the issues can assist in the search for solutions, since increasing awareness assists the Inuit and others to better define the problems that need to be addressed.

The origins of this book itself lie in an earlier awareness by Inuit of threats to their continued sustainable use of whales and other arctic living resources, threats that come from a variety of external forces and events. Thus, at the 1992 General Assembly of the Inuit Circumpolar Conference (ICC), a resolution was adopted that called upon the ICC Executive Board to commence an inquiry into the feasibility of assuming greater control over the management of whaling. The realization was widespread among the Inuit delegates from Alaska, Canada, Greenland, and Russia that, being a cultural minority situated far from the decision-making centres of industrialized and populous nations, they were unfairly victimized by the actions of wealthy and influential special interest groups close to the centres of political power.

Thus was launched an ICC inquiry seeking to document the significance of whales and whaling to Inuit in their homelands in Canada, Greenland, Russia, and the United States. Although the words of Inuit concerned with whales and whaling exist in many books, articles, and government reports, for the purposes of this book, we have relied only to a minimal extent on these available written sources. Rather, it was decided to seek out the current thoughts of Inuit—of all ages—living throughout the Inuit homelands. Thus, the authors of this report conducted and arranged interviews, requested teachers to encourage students to discuss and write on the topic, and generally focused on current perceptions and opinions. In addition, efforts were made, through cor-

FIGURE 1. Adult (white) and immature (grey) beluga whales, with walrus and seal, the principal Inuit food sources throughout most of the eastern Arctic. Grise Fiord, Canada, September 1965.

respondence, to obtain Inuit leaders' (and some governments') views on the whaling debate. The information gathered was extensive, and what is presented here is no more than a representative sample. All those whose words are used in this book understood that their words were to be used in this publication, and have consented to being identified; their remarks are unedited, except for length. At the end of each chapter a selection of further readings is provided.

Although this book focuses on the use and importance of various species of whales by Inuit at different times and places, to some extent such an emphasis on whales alone is somewhat misleading. Indeed, as a hunting people, the Inuit depend on a complex of resources in which whales (important as they are) comprise only one part. The reason for treating the Inuit–whale component of this complex in this disconnected fashion is that the call for this inquiry came in reaction to management concerns directed, more especially, at whaling alone.

It is a fact that national and international management arrangements are normally organized by categories that make sense to bureaucrats and specialists whose work has traditionally been organized in this compartmentalized fashion. Thus, in respect to questions about whaling, there exist the International Whaling Commission, the North Atlantic Marine Mammal Commission, the Canada–Greenland Joint Commission on Conservation and Management of Narwhal and Beluga, and the Alaska Eskimo Whaling Commission (all of which involve Inuit), as a few examples (among many) of how management concerns become separated, often for administrative convenience, from the integrated reality of the user community's life, experiences, needs, and understandings.

We would therefore stress the obvious: that Inuit whaling and other aspects of the Inuit–whale relationship occur in the rich context of a hunting, fishing, and gathering way of life that involves a large number of other arctic resources. These resource categories include seals (of several species), walrus, polar bear, caribou, reindeer, and many different wildfowl, as well as eggs, berries, fish, and shellfish (to name but a few of the resource categories). The diversity of habitats that Inuit occupy today, and that they have occupied in earlier times, make generalizations about human ecological relationships (and diet as an important expression of that relationship) difficult and sometimes unhelpful. For example, the relatively small numbers of Inuit living inland (in Alaska and Canada) will clearly have less dependence on marine mammals than those dwelling on the coast, whereas those in the far north (of Canada and Greenland) will have far less access to fish, shellfish, berries, and wildfowl than will those Inuit living in lower latitudes.

In their regional variations, however, Inuit cultures are overwhelmingly based on marine mammal hunting and utilization. Today, as in the past, Inuit identify with their culture and continue to place high value on whales (and other local foods) as a necessary health-promoting and identity-maintaining food. Whales are important in part because, as a large-bodied animal, each whale landed contributes in great measure to the available food supply. However, just as importantly, whales contribute to community social solidarity, and hence collective security, due to the cooperation that is required to successfully hunt, process, and distribute the enormous quantity of useful product that each whale provides. Large whales, such as bowhead, fin, or humpback (weighing up to fifty tonnes), obviously require many people working cooperatively to catch and process. However, even the smaller beluga (weighing up to one tonne) were often taken in large-scale drives involving dozens of hunters working in a highly coordinated and cooperative manner. The leadership required in such activities also serves to validate the status and continuing importance to society of older, more experienced, hunters. This validation is particularly important today, where elders' knowledge is sometimes deemed

FIGURE 2. Community members haul a bowhead whale ashore (note slabs of mattak placed on log platform in foreground). Shingle Point, Canada, September 1991.

less relevant in a fast-changing world that increasingly appears to be shaped by the values of the younger generation and outside agencies.

Among the external, nontraditional, events impacting Inuit society has been an increasing involvement with the market economy. Of course, this involvement is not new: in Greenland, local cash sale of country foods started in the early 1700s, and continues to this day. Elsewhere, Inuit were employed by American and European commercial whalers more than a century ago, with money as well as payments-in-kind (for example, boats, rifles, and other essentials) used to purchase their labour and skills. When large-scale commercial whaling ended in Alaska and Canada early this century, small-scale commercial whaling continued at several locations until quite recently, and for those not involved in these activities, furs, skins, ivory, and various handcrafted goods were traded and sold to obtain the imported goods Inuit needed to continue their hunting way of life.

Thus evolved the "mixed economy," an economy that combines traditional economic behaviour (such as sharing the product of the hunt without involving money) with selling and buying meat with money. The everyday use of cash occurs in all these contemporary wage-earning societies, where hunters sell their produce for cash to others, or where they receive cash contributions from others to help cover the cost of producing needed food, or where hunters can receive tax relief from the government to facilitate their continued hunting. Such mixed economies exist, in varying degrees, in all Inuit societies today; these commercial and noncommercial exchanges involve whale products as well as other tradeable items. One of the problems Inuit face today is attempts by opponents of whaling to ban the sale of edible whale products. However, the link between a healthy economy and a vibrant culture and society is self-evident, and, as pointed out by a 1997 World Conservation Union [IUCN] report, "... the degree of participation in the cash economy must be determined by the people themselves and on their own terms. This is what is known as the right to development. Only through recognition of this right can economic self-sufficiency and cultural autonomy be safeguarded."

Apart from the economic value of whale products as a trade item, and apart from its contribution to cultural autonomy, the importance of whales as a source of food cannot be underestimated. For not only is the mattak, oil, and meat highly regarded as a customary food, and hence eaten to satisfy aesthetic and emotional needs, but it also contributes in important nutritional ways to the physical health of the Inuit. The fact that Inuit of all ages almost everywhere regard mattak (the skin and underlying fatty tissue) as one of the most highly desired foods contributes to its social importance, for this great need ensures that hunters will continue to make the effort—even when conditions are severe—to hunt whales and assist others to learn the needed skills. This they will do in the knowledge that people will share their supply of mattak, knowing just how much others appreciate or need to receive it.

Scientific research continues to increase understanding of what has long been known about the nutritional importance of mattak, specifically its health-promoting qualities for Arctic peoples. Indeed, it has been known for several decades that fats derived from marine animals in general appear to protect against the various cardiovascular diseases that are a major cause of death among North Americans and Europeans. However, recent research suggests that the fatty acids contained in these marine oils provide only part of the reason for the almost complete absence of heart disease among Greenland Inuit. Mattak, it seems, is a major source of antioxidants (which keep the arteries healthy) and a highly enriched source of selenium, an element that also contributes to the antioxidation process. Selenium also appears to provide critical protection against the potentially harmful effects of mercury and other heavy metals that occur in varying amounts in local sources of food throughout the Arctic, and sometimes at higher levels than are considered safe under most developed nation's health guidelines.

Many factors across the Arctic have brought about, and will continue to bring about, change in the Inuit diet. Among these factors can be noted changing occupations and lifestyles, cultural changes resulting from schooling and satellite TV, and increased local availability of various imported foods, among many others. However, as mentioned earlier, among the most popular of locally produced foods (and as much as supplies allow), mattak remains a regular item of the diet. Mattak is popular, not just because it tastes good and is recognized as being healthy, but also because whales are recognized as being historically and culturally important animals. Hunting and consuming whales is the most appropriate way for members of a meat-eating hunting society to ensure that these historic and cultural connections are maintained and transmitted to succeeding generations.

Whales of various species, in some areas and times more than any other animal, have contributed greatly to Inuit survival; in the not-too-distant past, that survival was secured as much through rituals and religious observances as through technology and individual hunting skills. In those years, when the parents of today's elders were living, whales needed to come relatively close to land to be useful to the people on shore. It could be reasoned that killing a huge sea animal with handheld weapons, and then towing it to land, required the willingness of the animal to be taken—and assistance from forces greater than humans possessed to ensure that conditions allowed the hunt to be concluded safely. Thus whale hunting involved a number of ceremonies and ritual observances to show respect for this great animal, as well as gratitude for the animal's sacrifice at the conclusion of the hunt. Such observances and sense of gratitude and respect continue, in varying degree, to this day in Inuit whaling communities.

However, it must be stressed, and will be apparent in what follows, that Inuit whaling has always been adaptive—that is, it has changed through time in order to remain functional and socially, culturally, and economically important as conditions have changed. The most obvious evidence for such adaptiveness includes the technological changes that have occurred over time. When the American commercial whalers first sailed through the Bering Strait, they encountered Iñupiat hunting for bowhead from skin-covered boats with stone and bone hunting weapons. Almost immediately the Iñupiat recognized the advantages of using iron whaling implements, explosive harpoons, and rifles. The commercial whalers withdrew from the region after fifty or so years, leaving the Iñupiat with the new technology. However, today, bowhead hunters in Alaska continue using the same skin-covered boats their ancestors invented centuries before, for the simple reason that such craft remain the most effective boats for hunting whales under springtime conditions. At the same time, these Alaskan whalers use the iron tools and explosive harpoons introduced more than a century ago, but they also include in the whaling kit hand-held radios, snowmobiles, and now radio-equipped floats and more powerful (yet safer) explosive charges developed little more than a decade ago by Japanese and Norwegian commercial whaling interests. It is in the nature of people to seek a better life for themselves and their families, and arctic archaeology gives ample evidence of four thousand years of increasing Inuit technological innovation that we may confidently predict will continue far into the future.

Despite the increased security that improved technology and certain other features of modern living provide, various features of contemporary industrial civilization are not so beneficial. The effects of pollution, originating globally as well as locally, in some respects have a more worrisome effect in the northern latitudes—where the food production processes are quite different and more restricted than those in temperate or tropical regions. Originating in agricultural and industrial regions thousands of kilometres to the south, an alphabet soup of organochlorines (such as PCBs, PCCs, HCH, DDT, DDE, and so on), heavy metals, and radioactive isotopes eventually appear in the air, water, and tissues of arctic plants, animals, and people.

One definition of pollution is that it represents "material that is out of place." If that is so, then there is another form of pollution that is equally threatening to Inuit well-being. This is the mind pollution taking place in decision-making centres far distant from Inuit homelands, but that nevertheless represents a more immediate and severe threat than do PCBs, methylmercury, or radioactivity. This pollution involves the spread of extreme and—for a hunting people—out-of-place ideas promoted by animal protection organizations that assert that the human use of animals is perverse and unnecessary.

One of these reactionary ideas, which finds particular favour among city dwellers and politicians in some of the most ruthlessly capitalistic and environmentally damaging societies on the globe, is the notion that selling animal products for money constitutes a crime against nature. Unfounded and extreme as such generalizations are, in various guises they are uncritically embraced by bureaucrats and politicians in Brussels, London, Washington, D.C., and other national capitals far—in both distance and understanding—from northern realities. It is both ironic and tragic that it is the people and their understandings closest to nature who are subject to attack by those farthest removed from nature.

Rural and indigenous peoples are, in a sense, locked in battle with the industrialized world, as well as with the global processes of urbanization and the homogenization of cultures that such a world order induces. However, the industrialized world may have much to learn from Inuit and other indigenous peoples who have the philosophies, the practical knowledge, and the continued contact with nature's reality to better comprehend how to use renewable resources in a sustainable manner. The knowledge and attitudes that Inuit have developed and tested over time are a treasure they are willing to share with the rest of humankind. Yet, as opportunities are foreclosed for Inuit societies to adapt, on their own terms, to changing times and circumstances, continual loss of skills and knowledge that have served these people so well for so long are also in danger of being lost. This potential for loss is certainly increased as the economic viability of Inuit communities is weakened by legislated trade barriers crafted in ignorance of, and indifference to, the human costs that such damaging barriers impose.

In small part, this book seeks to reduce this ignorance. It is an acknowledgment, indeed a celebration, of the enduring relationship between Inuit and whales—a relationship that has lessons to offer humankind in our ongoing efforts to improve our collective ecological security.

[There is] misunderstanding about how the Inuit live, the way [we] think about whales. . . . How can we be misunderstood? How comes they don't understand us, since we can understand them, the way they live?. . . . People have to understand each other and have respect for each other. I think that is very important, because if you don't respect and understand the other people, you are going to be hurting someone out there very badly . . . in time people will understand why we hunt whales.

Johnny Mike, Pangnirtung, March 1995

CHAPTER ONE

—+ ⛩ +—

The Importance of Inuit Whaling Today

[Bowhead whales] were very essential to the lives of the Inuit. The Inuit at Ummangjuaq were "thirsty" when it came to the bowhead whales. . . . Those Inuit were hungry for bowhead mattak. . . . I think it is essential that we learn about the bowhead whale, how it tastes and its other uses.

Lypa Pitsiulak, Pangnirtung, April 1995

Whaling does not only provide food. There is also a wealth of traditions . . . hunters believe that a real man is the one who takes part in whaling. The whale festival is well known, which among the Naukan Yup'iit [Siberian Inuit] lasts about a month. Very much in the spiritual life of our people is determined by whaling . . . without whaling, there are no Yup'iit.

Tatyana Achirgina, Anadyr, 1995

Inuit hunt whales to fulfill a number of social, economic, cultural, and nutritional needs. The mattak and meat are important food sources in most Inuit communities and are widely used in gift-giving and intersettlement trade. In Canada and Greenland, narwhal ivory provides some hunters with needed cash income, as do various handicraft items fashioned from whale bone, teeth, and baleen. However, apart from its present-day material importance, whaling also serves to link Inuit symbolically and spiritually to their cultural heritage. Whale mattak remains, for the Inuit, one of the most highly desired traditional foods. Not only is mattak nutritionally and psychologically beneficial, but its widespread sharing among relatives and between communities creates and sustains the bonds that remain the basis of Inuit social and economic relationships in the North today.

These relationships are indeed critical to Inuit cultural survival. As the use of rifles became widespread in the nineteenth century, most types of hunting

FIGURE 3. Hunter using a scale selling narwhal meat to a customer. Qaanaaq, Greenland, August 1988.

(which were formerly a collective activity) became progressively more individualized. However, whaling continues to remain one of the most important collective hunting activities in many Inuit communities, and serves to continually reinforce significant culturally established collective rights and social relationships, responsibilities, and obligations.

SOCIAL IMPORTANCE

> In our society, the whaling captains are leaders. . . . A whaling captain is respected, he's a leader, he has to be able to be a leader in order to go out hunting, he's got to lead his crew, and he's got to lead the community in ceremonies.
>
> *Marie Adams, Barrow, 1983*

FIGURE 4. Cutting up a bowhead whale on the sea ice. Barrow, Alaska, May 1988.

During whale hunts, traditional social order is expressed when the eldest and most experienced hunters assume their roles as leaders and decision-makers for the group. Elders are also given special portions of whale meat or mattak as a sign of respect and affection, thus reaffirming their traditional role in Inuit society. In an increasingly changing world, Inuit whaling reaffirms traditional social, economic, and cultural norms through the hunt and the widespread sharing of meat and mattak.

In Alaska, hunting of the large bowhead and gray whale has resulted in a highly elaborate whaling culture in which the organization of boat crews reinforces kin relations within and between families and households in the community. This serves to link members of communities into effective networks that strengthen cooperation and social solidarity. The whaleboat captain (*umialiq*) occupies the most prestigious position in this social arrangement:

A whaling captain is faced with great responsibility. His number one priority is, of course, the immediate concerns of safety while out on the hazardous and icy arctic waters. Moreover, he is concerned with the sustenance of his people. It is his knowledge and preparation that the people depend upon for their daily food. A whaling captain is also charged with the preservation of the great bowhead whale. This duty and responsibility of preservation of the whale has been handed down from time immemorial.

Burton Rexford, Barrow

I often ask myself that same question . . . why did I become a whaling captain? Because of the opportunity to feed the community . . . The whale basically to me is a community whale. I get my share like everybody else, but you have the honour of feeding your community after a whale is caught. And the sharing . . . is where the attributes of culture haven't changed. . . . It's not that we go whaling for individual gain; it is for community gain.

Don Long, Barrow, April 1995

Sharing food is a basic ethic in Inuit society, and instills a feeling of social solidarity. A sense of community, fostered by widespread sharing, remains important in small and often remote communities where the necessities of life may sometimes be in short supply. Sharing mattak has special significance among all Inuit, because it is so highly valued by everyone. Whales, the largest animals hunted by Inuit, allow, to the greatest extent possible, expression of the importance of sharing food:

Each whale has tons of food that is shared to the entire village. . . . At [Barrow] the crews always share the whales with the villages of Nuiqsut, Wainwright, and Anaktuvuk Pass, and even with relatives and friends in places like Fairbanks and Anchorage.

Ralf Ahkivgak, Barrow, 1980

Thus when bowhead whaling resumed in the western Canadian Arctic (in 1991), the successful hunters ensured that meat and mattak was widely dispersed throughout neighbouring communities:

We always share here with our neighbours even if we only have a small amount. . . . [We] all want the bowhead mattak and meat. We share food with those who don't have it. . . . We will distribute the meat to any of the communities that want it. We always share our food.

Dorothy Arey, Aklavik, August 1991

Nevertheless, despite the best efforts to distribute the bowhead widely, the following letter appeared in the western Arctic newspaper, *Tusaayaksat* (December 20, 1991):

As you are aware, there are a number of Inuvialuit students who are attending school in the Yukon, Northwest Territories and southern Canada and who have missed out on the historic bowhead harvest, and are not receiving any of the mattak which is being distributed throughout the Inuvialuit Settlement Region. . . . I would appreciate being informed why we haven't been receiving what should be our share.

John Muffa Kudlak, Yellowknife

Similarly, when a bowhead was landed in 1994, a rare event in the eastern Canadian Arctic, widespread distribution of meat and mattak to neighbouring communities occurred. A student explains:

The three men who killed the bowhead [did so] because an elderly man who was dying wanted to taste the meat one more time before he died. The meat from this whale was shared with the people of that community as well as other communities, including here in Pangnirtung.

Sheena Machmer, Attagoyak School, Pangnirtung, February 1995

In a study of hunting at Point Hope, Alaska, it was explained that the ethic of generosity was vitally important to each whaling captain because everyone soon knows when an individual is being less generous, and a poor reputation in that regard will certainly create difficulty in recruiting a good whaling crew in subsequent years. The study quotes a Point Hope whaling captain:

What's the point of catching a whale if I don't just give away as much of it as I can? There's no joy in doing this just for myself, you know. The people are hungry for their whale meat. I don't mind what qalgi [ceremonial men's house] they come from. . . . When it comes to a whale I catch, we're all one people.

Quoted in Tom Lowenstein, "Some Aspects of Sea Ice
Subsistence Hunting in Point Hope, Alaska," n.d.

Even smaller whales, the beluga and narwhal, allow Inuit to express in appropriate measure the important act of sharing food:

. . . whenever someone gets a whale the people gather down on the beach. Everyone would get some food to bring back home. People usually gather at a home . . . to get more mattak. These gatherings and sharings are as much a part of our culture as [is] our language.

Oolletoa Temela, Qaqqalik School, Lake Harbour, March 1995

FIGURE 5. Community members receiving beluga whale shares. Belcher Islands, Canada, July 1960.

> When a whale is caught it's shared with the whole community. Whales provide a lot of food. There is lots to go around. Some families do not get whales so other families will share their whale with them. This tradition always will be around in our community.
>
> *Charlie Novalinga, Nuiyak School, Sanikiluaq, March 1995*

Although it is generally the men who kill the whale, nevertheless the importance of women in whaling is well recognized among the Inuit:

> The whaling captain's wife is like a general. Her responsibilities are so great that the captain doesn't go out to seek the whale. . . . The captain's wife . . . is the main catcher. . . . She "brings in" the whale. . . . She makes it easier for the captain to harvest a whale, but the woman has to be in a proper state of mind because she is actually the "bearer" of the crew and is called a "crew captain." The women who stay at home with the children and the family along with the whole community are what I call "callers of whales."
>
> *Frank Long Jr., Nuiqsut, March 1994*

During the whaling symposium at which Frank Long Jr. spoke, whaling captains from Point Hope and Barrow also confirmed that in their communities women are designated as captains. In a recent study of Iñupiat whaling, Ernie

Frankson, a Point Hope hunter, corrects the anthropologist's statement that "only men hunt" by reminding her: *the whale comes to the whaling captain's wife.*"

WHALES AS A SOURCE OF FOOD

For hundreds of years the Inuit have hunted whales for food. This is the most important aspect of whale hunting. Inuit depend on whales and other marine mammals for food. This food is part of the Inuit diet, as well as their bodies, blood and heart.

Sheena Machmer, Attagoyak School, Pangnirtung, February 1995

For most Inuit, marine mammals are considered the most important sources of food. Whales, being among the largest of the marine mammals, are clearly important in terms of the quantity of varied and esteemed foods, as well as the abundance of oil. Even in the few noncoastal Inuit communities in Alaska and Canada, people expect to obtain whale from their relatives living on the coast:

I am not a whale hunter . . . I am only an inland hunter . . . even though I am not a whale hunter I was raised on blubber and oil with meat. . . . I would hear that Barrow people had caught a whale and, yes . . . I will eat oil from that whale. . . . My relatives will send me some mattak and meat. . . . Whenever Barrow catches a whale, it doesn't matter which crew, a package will reach us with mattak and meat.

Elijah Kakinya, Anaktuvuk Pass, September 1977

Elsewhere, throughout the Arctic, Inuit regard whales as a highly valued food resource:

Whaling for narwhal and beluga is a part of our life. It is very special to us because we make dried meat from whales. We dry meat for our winter food supply. Some of the narwhal is preserved under stones near the hunting areas where we catch the whales. We then fetch it in winter for our own food and for our dogs.

Ussarqak Qujaukitsoq, Qaanaaq, July 1995

For our village . . . it is very important to take whales. . . . The whale feeds the entire village, and there is no-one who goes to sleep hungry.

Sergei Rentin and Yurii Yatta, New Chaplino, October 1995

FIGURE 6.   Drying narwhal meat at Qaanaaq, Greenland, August 1988.

Whales and sea mammals are considered to be the best food to feed the [Inuit] body. . . . Without these types of foods, we, the Inuit, would have been gone a long time ago. Therefore, in order to live a full and healthy life and to keep the generations going, we, the Inuit, need the food that has brought us to where we are today.

Angela Gibbons, Sakku School, Coral Harbour, March 1995

Not only do these customary foods form part of the diet, but in many respects they are irreplaceable, for many Inuit find that imported foods cannot provide suitable substitutes. During public hearings held in Barrow in connection with proposed oil and gas industry activities, many hunters expressed their concern that industrial activities would harm the whales and consequently the basis of their food supply:

Even though I have a white man for a father, my stomach is an Inupiaq stomach. Without [whale and seal] oil, without fermented Inupiaq meat, I couldn't live . . . ever.

T. Brower, Sr., Barrow, 1983

Those elders would become sick if they were forced to quit eating something which they had eaten ever since they were very little.

A. Solomon, Barrow, 1983

[Even] if they stop us, I'm going to take my boat and go whale hunting. I have to have it for food; it is part of my body.

E. Brower, Barrow, 1983

Such sentiments continue to be expressed because the cultural and emotional connections to a customary diet do not easily erode, especially in a society where sharing ensures that, even when food is in short supply, no one is denied the food they need:

[Bowheads] are very important for nutrition up here. . . . People think that because we have jobs that maybe it isn't as important, but people like myself grew up on Native food and we're not accustomed to butter and beef and chicken fat. All that stuff makes me sick.

Marie Adams Carroll, Barrow, 1995

The privation elders feel when denied customary food that embodies such social and cultural significance is well understood, even by younger members of society, as this poignant account by a young student attests:

I recall as a young child visiting my grandparents' house. . . . One conversation is still alive in my memory. My grandparents and many relatives were gathered and eating mataaq [beluga mattak] when my grandfather sighed and said to himself . . . "just one more time before I die." I did not understand what this meant; then I understood, for my grandmother turned to him and said, "One day we will eat, one day there will be bowhead meat for us." I've heard many more conversations similar to the one between my grandparents, but none in all my fifteen years were as memorable and sad. . . . Many elders have passed on without tasting their beloved mataq [bowhead mattak] one more time.

Adina Duffy, Sakku School, Coral Harbour, March 1995

If the authorities delay issuing licences for [bowhead] hunting, our grandmothers and grandfathers will go without tasting the bowhead meat. That would be bad for them and that would be bad for us too, for we would not have been able to do right by them.

Petr Typykhkak, Sireniki, February 1996

No one sent up mattak for Thanksgiving this year. It was a sad, sad time. I only pray to God for a little bit of mattak at Christmas, just a little taste. That would make my heart happy.

Barrow elder, 1983

There are not words for the emptiness I would feel if we didn't have mattak to share at our feasts. I could not even imagine such a thing, it is so much a part of me.

Point Hope elder, 1983

This desire for whale mattak and meat remains very strong in Inuit society today. A study of food preference carried out in Aklavik in 1991 indicated that on a scale of 1 (low preference) to 5 (high preference), beluga mattak was rated 4.9 by a representative sample of adults and 4.6 by schoolchildren. Beluga dried meat was rated higher by children than by adults (4.7 and 4.5 respectively). Aklavik is a riverine community, about 130 km from the coast, yet beluga was the second-most frequently eaten food (after caribou) out of more than forty different local food species eaten during each year. A 1995 public health study in Greenland found that mattak was at the top of the list of preferred foods eaten by men, with imported foods (pork, chicken, and sausage) at the bottom.

In 1994, a national survey in Greenland found that, in the towns, only about 13 percent of households answered "seldom or never" when asked how often the main meat in their diet was local, Greenlandic, food; in the settlements outside of the main urban areas, the figure was 3 percent. The majority of Greenland households (41 percent in towns and 78 percent in the settlements) ate local meat three or four times per week, or more often than that.

CULTURAL IMPORTANCE

The reason I'm here today is because my father, grandfather, and great-grandfather survived on whales. . . . We need to keep our tradition alive and strong.

Charlie Novalinga, Nuiyak School, Sanikiluaq, March 1995

Whales and whaling are common themes in the songs, legends, toponymy, art, dance, and the thoughts of Inuit everywhere, even among youth; the arrival of migrating whales in the spring is a highlight of the annual calendar. The whale, as food, has cultural as well as physiological importance, for it meets enduring aesthetic, emotional, and symbolic needs:

If the right to hunt is taken away, the Inuit will die, either physically or emotionally. I say emotionally because the Inuit will crave for the food which they have lost and they will feel as though they have let their ancestors' culture disappear. They will start to feel ashamed of having been an Inuk, which may lead to having no respect for their ancestors.

Angela Gibbons, Sakku School, Coral Harbour, March 1995

My grandfather had grown up with the taste of bowhead whale. . . . He hunted them, he ate them, he craved them. I believe that the prohibition on hunting the bowhead took something away from the Inuit that can never be returned.

Adina Duffy, Sakku School, Coral Harbour, March 1995

Perspectives such as these are expressed wherever Inuit live. In varying, but ever-present degree, whatever the age or occupational preferences of those speaking, "we are what we eat" is today, as it was in the past, a truism heard in almost every human society and culture. This is certainly the case among the Inuit:

[Although] I have learned more about the white man's ways . . . I am still Inuk because I grew up on Inuk food.

Mosesie Idlout, Resolute, 1975

But everyone in Resolute is dependent on hunting and whaling. Not only do we like our own food better than the white man's, but we can't afford to live from the white man's food. . . . That's why it is so important for us to protect our own food. . . . Our hunting, our land and our lives are intimately connected; they cannot be separated.

Walter Audla, Resolute, 1983

This is the way I think. A person is born with animals. He has to eat animals. That is why the animals and a person are just like one.

Peter Okpik, Gjoa Haven, 1975

Whales are very important to the people who eat whales. . . . Once we don't have the whales' nutrients in our bodies, it's like part of our bodies is missing.

Tina Netser, Sakku School, Coral Harbour, March 1995

When a hunter kills a whale, the meat is never wasted. Everyone gets a piece of the whale for their family. God put them there for a reason, and the people use it wisely. . . . If the people do have too much, they give the leftovers to the people who need it.

Student, Maani Uluyuk School, Rankin Inlet, February 1995

Sharing animals is an important cultural value. For Inuit, it reflects more than human dependence on animals for essential food and materials. Indeed, it reaffirms the interdependence between humans and animals. This mutual dependence is based on the separate, but complementary, needs of people and animals, needs that each is able to satisfy for the other. Long ago, Inuit came to understand that animals provide people with the necessities of life in this world, and people, by observing the appropriate rituals and etiquette when animals are killed and consumed, are able to ensure that animal populations will remain healthy and ever-present. The destiny of animals is to sustain people through the gifts that their bodies provide—the gifts of bones for tools, skins for clothing, flesh for food, and oil for eating, heating, and lighting. However, to guarantee future supplies of these necessities of life, appropriate behaviour is required from humans when acquiring, sharing, and consuming these gifts, in order to ensure that the individual animal's destiny is adequately fulfilled.

Thus, there are many rules and observances that have come to govern Inuit–whale relationships over the years. The anthropologist Franz Boas, in the 1880s, observed that Baffin Island Inuit, after a whale had been killed, could not hunt another whale for at least five days. Knud Rasmussen, following his visit to the Igloolik people in the early 1920s, describes many such observances intended to show respect for whales, including this particular one:

> During a whale hunt, the women were obliged to wear a head ornament consisting of a white quartzite, fastened to a strap round the forehead. This was done to show a light for the soul of the whale.

Today, certain of these observances of the past continue to be part of Inuit life:

> At Point Hope every part of the whale is used for the community and the only part of the whale that is put back into the ocean is the skull. And when we do that, that tells us that the spirit is good and in the next spring another whale will be coming back to the community to be used as food. And when we throw that head into the water, we have a joyful moment.
> *Elijah Rock, Point Hope, March 1994*

> After landing the dead beluga on the ice . . . the hunters put some of the blood back into the ocean right away. After cutting the beluga open, a piece of liver is also thrown into the sea. When butchering is finished, the head and organs—except the heart—are returned to the sea. In this way the animal returns to the open sea . . . by doing this, the hunters ensure the animals will come again.
> *Konstantin Kymyechgin, Yanrakinnot, October 1996*

Among other ways whales are treated with respect is by ensuring orderliness and cleanliness in connection with their treatment. Following a bowhead hunt in the western Canadian Arctic in 1991, the local newspaper (*Tusaayaksat*, September 20, 1991) reported: "Most people left [the whaling camp] by Sunday, but Captain Danny A. Gordon stayed until Monday, the last person at Shingle, making sure the site was cleaned up and left as they had found it a month earlier when preparations for the historic hunt began." In the hunt captain's own words at the time:

> We have cut it all up, as you can see; all the mattak and meat . . . it will be shared out. We'll leave the bones here for the animals. It will all be cleaned up in no time. There are lots of [scavenging] animals around here birds, polar bears, grizzlies, wolves, white fox, red fox, wolverine.
> *Danny A. Gordon, Aklavik, September 1991*

Although some of the many rules, ceremonies, and rituals are no longer practiced as they once were, they may continue to be kept alive in stories, songs, and dance. Elsewhere, hunters continue to practice the timeless rituals as did their fathers and generations before, and mothers pass on the customary etiquette within the household. These practices comprise the essential elements of a distinctive and respected culture, one that many Inuit believe passionately should be maintained, for the preservation of that culture, for love of the elders alive today, and out of a sense of duty and respect to those who went before:

> We still want to live like before, just for our elders. Elders are big helpers to us. All Inuit feel all the same to[ward] the whaling issue. . . . Inuit culture is something big for us.
> *Debbie Kriterdluk, Maani Ulujuk School, Rankin Inlet, February 1995*

> We ourselves should think of the preservation of the most ancient culture—marine hunting—which is the basis of life, culture, and the language of coastal dwellers of Chukotka. We should ensure our survival as unique peoples and pass the experience and traditional mode of life over to our descendants.
> *Lyudmila Ainana (Chairman, Eskimo Society of Chukotka), Tatyana Achirgina (Vice President–Chukotka, Inuit Circumpolar Conference) and others, March 1995*

> Whaling should be developed today and preserved for the future . . . otherwise we shall . . . lose our identity. . . . So whaling is essential to the preservation of the traditional culture; if we continue to whale, dress, sew, and process [whales], we shall retain our uniqueness.
> *Lyubov Piskunova, Lorino, April 1995*

FIGURE 7. Elders being recognized at a community feast to celebrate a successful bowhead hunt. Aklavik, Canada, September 1991.

This strong attachment to hunting, and to the continued use of the products of the hunt, permeates all aspects of Inuit society. It is understandable and expected that adults would feel this attachment, for in many cases their early lives were, to a greater extent than today, spent living on the animals:

> We have to go out and get [food]. . . . I just can't go to the store and pick it up. . . . [Our] relationship to the land is very important because the land is alive, the animals and the sea itself; and you are interacting [with them]. . . . Going to catch a whale, the feeling that you get is never what you get going down to the store. Going down to the store, you're on dead ground: all the buildings are dead. All the items in there are dead, there's nothing alive . . . but here in the North, it's a lot more. . . . You're not only just going there just for food, you're going there to interact with nature, to understand more of these animals. A whale gives of itself: it's an animal that you feel fully about, it's something that gives itself up to you and that's an important thing in our beliefs, that's still very strong.
>
> *Simionie Akpalialuk, Pangnirtung, March 1995*

Throughout the Arctic, young Inuit live in modern communities, attend schools where teachers are mostly non-Inuit, and watch satellite TV programmes that glorify foreign values. Nevertheless, many of these young people under-stand what Inuit of Simionie Akpalialuk's generation are speaking about:

> When I say joy of hunting, white people think "Oh, the man thing!" to prove you are a man? No, that's not what it is; the joy of killing an animal is that you know someone will be happy to eat the gift from the Earth. We are not macho types, like what some of you think we are.
>
> *Koochy Kolala, Qaqqalik School, Lake Harbour, March 1995*

So despite diverse cultural influences impacting on the younger people's values and perceptions, many young people continue to express profound attachment to Inuit culture and are determined to help it survive:

> I just want to say that whaling on the Hudson Bay is already a major part of my life even though I am still young. I've been hunting whales ever since I can remember, with my grandpa, dad, uncles and many other relatives. . . . Whaling plays a major role in most Inuit lives. . . . If it's hunting, cooking or eating [animals], it is important to Inuit culture.
>
> *Neco Towtongie, Maani Ulujuk School, Rankin Inlet, February 1995*

FIGURE 8. Schoolchildren watching a community bowhead hunt on film. Aklavik, Canada, October 1991.

My grandmother's father was a whaler, way before I was here; she tells me stories about how important the whales were to them, and how important they are to us, and the culture and the traditions . . . please don't take that away from us.

Pauline Kudluk, Sakku School, Coral Harbour, March 1995

In my family, my great-great-great grandfather Angmarlik was a whaling leader and . . . was involved in a lot of hunting for whales, especially bowhead whales. Then my great-great-grandfather Qatuuq was in whaling too; he helped and killed bowhead whales. Then my great-grandfather Leah was a Scottish whaler, and he was involved with whaling too. By the time my grandfather Geela was old enough to hunt . . . bowhead hunting was no longer allowed. Now my father Joopa is a hunter. . . . I am also old enough to hunt, but again, I cannot hunt bowhead. As the future generations grow, if this continues, our traditional ways of whaling will be lost forever. Everyone who knows whaling will have passed away and there will be no-one to teach us and our children how to hunt whales.

Leesa Sowdluapik, Attagoyak School Pangnirtung, February 1995

FIGURE 9. Bowhead whale landed at Pangnirtung, Canada, 1945.

NUTRITION AND HEALTH

When it's been a long time since [my mother] had Inuit food she gets weak, and only gets better when she eats Inuit food. A lot of Inuit are like my mother. They need their type of food to keep their strength. We depend on whales and other marine mammals for strength.

Sheena Machmer, Attagoyak School, Pangnirtung, February 1995

When considering whales as food, Inuit emphasize the health-promoting properties of the oil, blubber, and fresh meat:

An Inupiaq cannot satisfy his hunger without oil even though he is eating other things too. . . . I was raised on oil, because my father was a concerned provider who also couldn't go without oil. This is so for our people; nobody here can live without oil. . . . Come lunch time it must be there and also at suppertime. . . . I am 82 years old and my wife is 81, because both of us know how to treat our stomachs.

Elijah Kakinya, Barrow, September 1977

We, as Inuit, our tradition is fresh meat, and I know that it can keep the body in shape. . . . Only animals keep us strong as Inuit. . . . When we haven't taken seal blubber for a while, we weaken. . . . When we haven't eaten fresh meat for a while, we get really tired. And then, when we do eat it, our body gets satisfied because we are Inuit. . . . Even if we eat white man's food, if we haven't eaten Inuit food for a while, we weaken.

Anonymous Inuk, Sanikiluaq, reported in Usher et al. 1995

Scientific studies confirm the superior nutritional value of whale and other local foods compared to store-bought imported foods such as beef, pork, or chicken. Danish and Norwegian physicians and scientists were among the first to study the nutritional value of the Inuit diet. Among their findings was the conclusion that whale mattak, long known to provide excellent protection against scurvy, contains rich sources of vitamins A and C, thiamin, riboflavin, and niacin.

COMPOSITION OF BEEF AND WHALE MEAT AND MATTAK

	Protein (gm/100)	Fat (gm/100)	Vitamin A IUs	Riboflavin (mg)	Niacin (mg)	Iron (mg)	Phosphorus (mg)
Beef	16.5	28	60	0.15	4.0	2.5	152
Bowhead	23.9	1.6	330	0.55	7.4	14.0	212
Beluga (meat)	24.5	0.5	335	0.40	6.8	26.6	270
Beluga (mattak)	27.0	4.2	N/A	N/A	N/A	0.4	202

(From: U.S. Department of Agriculture and U.S. Department of Health, Education, and Welfare)

The importance for Inuit of maintaining high intake levels of iron is indicated by low blood-iron levels found among Inuit workers at mine sites in the north who ate regular mess-hall meals of red (but blood-drained) beef. Inuit recognize the importance of blood in their diet. In commenting on meat processed in industrial slaughterhouses, one Inuk commented:

> You eat it, then you get hungry, like half an hour after you eat it. Where[as] when you eat meat with blood in it at lunch, you're good for the whole day. All you have to do is drink lots of tea all day after that. Never really have to eat again. They couldn't do that with that [store food].
>
> *Anonymous Inuk, Sanikiluaq, quoted in Usher et al. 1995*

> It's the animal's blood that gives us strength. . . . Blood is very good for the body. . . . Because it's very good, the seal's blood keeps us healthy. The animal's blood is very good, very good. . . . It prevents sickness easier, too. . . . We say to children, "Eat fresh meat so you won't be sick" and we set an example so they themselves will follow our ways.
>
> *Anonymous Inuk, Sanikiluaq, quoted in Usher et al. 1995*

> When one eats meat, it warms your body very quickly. But when one eats fruit or other imported food, it doesn't help keep you very warm. With imported food . . . you're warm just a short time. But [our] meat is different; it keeps you warm. It doesn't matter if it is raw meat or frozen meat . . . it has the same effect.
>
> *Ussarqak Qujaukitsoq, Qaanaaq, July 1995*

Apart from the meat and blood, the fat component of whale is especially important, for marine mammal fats are low in saturated fats and high in the omega-3 polyunsaturated fatty acids that offer protection from the cardiovascular diseases common in North America and Europe. Indeed, it was the low incidence of heart disease among Greenlanders, despite their high-fat diet, that resulted in the beneficial effects of omega-3 fatty acids becoming known to science through the work of Drs. Bang and Dyerberg in West Greenland hunting communities.

More recently, the relationship between omega-3 polyunsaturated fatty acids and heart disease has been shown to be more complex than first believed. This new understanding arose because of the observation that Europeans and some Alaskan aboriginal peoples who include a high proportion of marine fish in their diets (and therefore should be well protected against heart disease) still have higher rates of disease than do Greenlanders. It is now believed that it is a combination of omega-3 polyunsaturated fatty acids, monounsaturated fatty acids, and antioxidants working together that reduces cholesterol and prevents sclerosis of the arteries. Selenium has been identified as an important antioxidant occurring in arctic diets, and as Dr. J. C. Hansen (of the Centre of Arctic Environmental Medicine, Aarhus University) and his colleagues noted in a 1994 review of the scientific evidence: "the richest source of selenium in Greenland is whaleskin, mattak." To Inuit, the beneficial effects of continuing to eat their customary diet are self-evident, as well as remedying to the difficulty elders experience when eating substitute foods:

> The nutritional value of whales is very important to people. It has vitamins and no preservatives or [refined] sugar. . . . Whales are fresh and healthy. . . . Our elders could get sick from retail food because [it] has a lot of sugar and other things that are not healthy. . . . Whales make a lot of people healthy. Elders would suffer [without them] because they've been eating whales since they were born.
>
> *Isobell Tukatuk, Nuiyak School, Sanikiluaq, March 1995*

> Our old men should by all means taste the meat and mattak of [the bowhead], the main prey of the Yup'iit. . . . The correct traditional nutrition is vital to the preservation of [our] health. In this respect, the meat of the whales and other marine mammals is exactly what is saving us.
>
> *Lyudmila Ainana, Provideniya, 1995*

Whales and sea mammals are considered to be the best food to feed the [Inuit] body. . . . Without these types of foods, we the Inuit would have been gone a long time ago. Therefore, in order to live a full and healthy life and to keep the generations going, we, the Inuit, need the food that has brought us to where we are today.

Angela Gibbons, Sakku School, Coral Harbour, March 1995

In a report to the International Whaling Commission (IWC) in 1989, the Greenland Home Rule authorities repeated the conclusion of a 1984 IWC report that warned against substituting a Euro-American diet for the traditional Inuit diet, stating: *"any transition away from the traditional Greenland diet will entail a risk of introduction of diet-related civilizational diseases in Greenland."* The 1989 report explained that these "diseases of civilization" (for example, heart disease and strokes, gallbladder disease, diabetes, and various neoplasms) *"are the end result of industrially produced highly specialized foodstuffs with their high content of simple carbohydrates, as well as the high content of fat with a low component of poly-unsaturated fatty acids."*

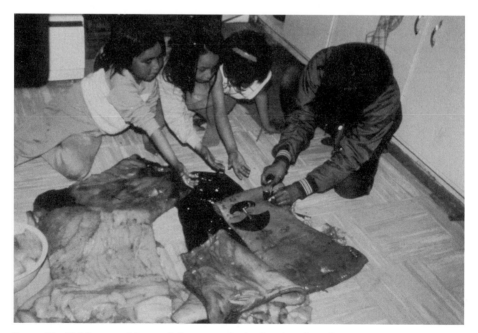

FIGURE 10. Children snacking on beluga mattak. Arviat, Canada, July 1986.

ECONOMIC IMPORTANCE

I stuck all the tail portion in my [ice] cellar. . . . I use it up for the feasts, Nalukataq, Christmas, Thanksgiving . . . that's what everyone does. That's what we believe: it's not mine—I'm just taking care of it.

Barrow whaling captain, April 1995

Economic transactions occurring within small-scale communities always possess social meaning. This is true whether such transactions involve gifts, bartered items, or the exchange of items for cash. Indeed, the exchange of goods, services, and money in these societies allows them to maintain the relations and processes of production that are deeply rooted, and hence meaningful, to community members' traditions and cultural identity.

We have practiced barter for hundreds of years. [But] in our times, money has appeared. . . . Hence I believe that we are entitled to sell some part of the whaling product. . . . Otherwise how are we going to survive? Of course, an exchange with reindeer herders should remain. It is part of our traditional economy.

Lyudmila Ainana, Provideniya, 1995

In the Inuit homelands, varying levels of commodification of whale products occur, depending on such factors as local economic circumstances of particular communities or regions, national legislation affecting the sale of game products, and historic circumstances shaping local interactions with regional or metropolitan markets. The importance of these varying circumstances is recognized by some Inuit:

Bartering has been part of our tradition for many years. . . . Selling whale products, I think . . . that differs from region to region. . . . It would be easy for me to say I'm against sale of any whale meat or mattak, because up here that's not such a key issue. But in other places . . . I think it is better for Native people to eat whale meat and mattak than to eat Twinkies and beef steaks and chicken fat.

Marie Adams Carroll, Barrow, April 1995

If selling surplus local produce is unnecessary for maintaining the social and economic well-being of Inuit households in some areas, the situation is vastly different in other areas where employment and other economic opportunities may be more limited. For example:

> We have not been paid our wages for half a year, and we cannot afford to buy imported food. That is why we rely on marine mammal meat for food. In addition we sell the meat to the fur farm [to be fed to the foxes] and are paid in accordance with the weight. . . . It is profitable for us to harvest whales for numerous reasons. I think that in the future, the role of whale hunting will not decline, because it is hardly conceivable that [economic] reforms will make life easier for northern people. Hence, our families will continue to be supported by what we kill.
>
> *Sergei Penetegin, Lorino, May 1995*

In other areas, a market economy provides the most efficient and satisfactory way of moving surplus local foods from areas of production to areas elsewhere in which consumer demand for these customary foods exists. In Greenland, such a system has been in place since the late 1700s, and today a nationwide purchasing, distributing, and retailing system exists to serve several important functions, including improving the self-sufficiency and viability of small hunting communities, as well as decreasing the national dependence on costly and less nutritious imported foods. Greenlanders employed in towns, for example, would be unable to obtain readily the nutritionally and culturally required mattak, whale meat, and other sea mammal–derived foods unless these foods could be purchased locally. In 1993, hunters in Nuuk (where about 25 percent of Greenland's population lives) killed fifteen beluga and four narwhal—a combined catch that represented less than 3 percent of the Greenland catch of these two species. Yet a national system of distribution to retail stores ensures that residents of Nuuk (and other urban centres) have access to meat and mattak taken more readily in the hunting districts.

In his book *Arctic Wars: Animal Rights, Endangered Peoples*, Greenlandic scholar Finn Lynge provides this observation on the mixed economy existing in his country:

> Seals and whales are hunted for their meat, and the meat that is taken is distributed to everyone on land who is interested. The distribution is performed along guidelines based partly on the old rules about hunt shares and on the fact that many people who are not covered by these traditional regulations do want to have some of the meat and do have money. Money is needed by the hunters to buy many daily commodities. Money is the only means of exchange that can open the channels of distribution in a modern society. The fact is that everyone wants meat, but only a small part of the population lives in places where landing this meat is the general way of life. . . . The life of a hunter has changed in many ways since the old days . . . but the subsistence

lifestyle has survived and functions now as an integral part of a modern and partially industrialized society—without endangering its soul.

What is common to all Inuit areas is the continued importance of locally hunted foods; if that food is not hunted locally, it has to be purchased. In some areas, it might be possible to replace some of the nutritional value obtained from whales with that derived from other species of marine mammal or fish. However, this is not always possible. Nor is it always desirable from a conservation perspective, for it often makes sense to gather food from a larger, rather than from a smaller, variety of species to maintain local and regional biodiversity:

> [We] decided last year that we should seek [baleen whale] quotas of 800 metric tonnes . . . based on the fact that there have been restrictions placed on hunting of other species; for example, reindeer hunting has been stopped over the past two years. Murre hunting has also been sharply regulated, and the salmon fishery can only be used for subsistence. . . . Arctic char fishing has similarly become subject to strong regulations in the past ten years.
> *Anton Siegstad and Hansi Kreutzmann, Nuuk, May 1995*

It is quite probable that taking two tonnes of food in the form of one minke whale (from a population of minkes numbering in the thousands) does far less ecological damage than does taking 50 reindeer, or 1,000 char, or 5,000 murres (or some combination adding up to two tonnes of food) from local animal populations seemingly in need of strict protection for conservation reasons.

Generally speaking, whaling is extremely cost-effective compared to some alternative hunting methods, owing to the large size of the landed carcass. The cost of minke whale meat in local Greenlandic markets was between U.S. $5 and $6/kg in 1993–94, so that the commodity value of 800 tonnes of whale meat would be around $4.5 million. In addition to the meat and mattak of the larger species of whales entering the Greenland market, there is also the considerable economic value of the meat and mattak of around 2,500 small cetaceans (such as beluga, narwhal, porpoises, and pilot whales) also taken annually by Greenland hunters. The 1994 national survey in Greenland indicated that almost half the households purchased fresh local meat from the local market or directly from the hunter or fisher.

In the Canadian Arctic, only a small quantity of edible whale product, almost exclusively mattak, is sold. However, the financial cost of replacing the food value of the approximately 1,000 beluga and narwhal taken annually would be considerable, and would cause severe problems in many communities where jobs are scarce and disposable income is consequently limited. In

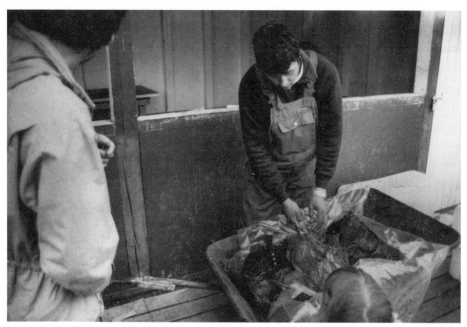

FIGURE 11. Hunter selling whale meat in the local market. Qeqertarsuaq, Greenland, 1995.

some communities, hunters are able to earn income by guiding sport hunters; however, regulations require that such hunts be carried out with dog teams. Whale meat and offal provide an important source of dog food in many eastern Arctic communities. In Nunavut, the replacement value of food obtained by hunting was estimated to total more than U.S. $62 million in 1989, a significant portion of which was obtained from whales and other marine mammals. More to the point, the absence of edible marine mammal products would place considerable stress on family incomes and on other local game populations, particularly caribou, as well as on several species of fish and wildfowl.

The replacement cost of the 1,000 tonnes of food provided from the fifty bowhead, and other whales, taken each year in Alaska would likely be about U.S. $10 million.

Elsewhere, however, alternatives to local food supplies just do not exist:

> . . . in the near future the importance of whaling will even increase. It is too important for the villages of the Providenskii and Chokotskii districts and coastal villages in the Iultin district. In fact, the Anadyr and Moscow authorities merely abandoned us: no food is brought [in] and we eat what hunters kill and women and children gather. The rural relatives help those who live in the district centres of Provideniya and Lavrentiya to survive.
>
> *Lyudmila Ainana, Provideniya, 1995*

WHALING AND SPIRITUALITY

Hunting is one of the most important traditions of the Inuit. . . . Whales, seals, walrus and all the other animals were put onto the earth for a reason and it is not right for anyone to take away what was brought into existence for a purpose.

Angela Gibbons, Sakku School, Coral Harbour, March 1995

Given a centuries-old dependence on the living resources, it is inevitable that Inuit social institutions and cultural beliefs would, over time, combine to make the human–animal relationship more secure, more enduring, and subject to greater human understanding. However, because nature sometimes acts against the best interests of even the most deserving of individuals, the human–animal relationship is affected by forces that may be hard to influence. Hence, the deep spirituality with which Inuit view their relationship with animals, the environment, and with nature in all its complexity.

Our body fluids are mixed with the blood of animals, with the oil of the animals. . . . Today, in the time of change in our lives, the Iñupiat, the white man, the animals—all three have one breath, they have one life. All three have the same source of living.

Patrick Attungana, Point Hope, February 1985

Such beliefs are widespread today, and connect with traditional understandings found throughout the Inuit homelands, as recorded in this 1922 statement by a Canadian Inuit shaman:

The greatest peril of life lies in the fact that human food consists entirely of souls.

Aua, Lyon Inlet, 1922

Knud Rasmussen, in his epic study *Intellectual Life of the Iglulik Eskimos*, placed Aua's words into an appropriate Inuit cultural context:

Animals have in reality no objection to being killed by human beings, as long as the rules of life are observed by the latter. It may even happen, and not infrequently, that an animal will approach a human being, actually desiring to be killed by that particular person. . . . The great danger in killing animals commonly hunted lies in the fact that there is hardly a single human being who has kept the rules of life and lived throughout in accordance with the laws laid down by the wisdom of his forefathers. Therefore it is said that the greatest danger lies in the fact that unclean and often guilty human beings have to depend entirely on the souls of other beings for food.

Today, similar concerns about respecting animals continue to be expressed:

Every so often we watch [TV] programs where there's people that are fishing . . . and I really disagree with that catch and release. I think that if you're going to go out there to fish, you get what you need and then leave the rest alone. . . . What harm are you bringing on these fish [if] they are being released?. . . . I really strongly disagree with people that are there to sport fish. . . .

> Ida McWilliam, interviewed by Angel Kuliktana on file
> with Kitikmeot Inuit Association, Kugluktuk, 1995

The Inuit . . . needed animals to survive; if they abused them they would have put their own lives in danger.

> Adina Duffy, Sakku School, Coral Harbour, March 1995

The norm of sharing is one very important way to show respect to animals, for sharing signifies generosity, which is a virtue, and an appropriate use for the gift of food the animal provides:

People are not cheap [stingy] with whales: the whole community shares the whale, they announce it on the radio. Then they tell the people to come and get the food. Every part of the whale is used. . . . We don't waste the whale, we use it all. We don't waste what we get.

> Isabell Tukatuk, Nuiyak School, Sanikiluaq, March 1995

The whale doesn't belong to me. It belongs to the community. . . . I am just a guardian of that whale for the winter—to distribute it to the community.

> Don Long, Barrow, April 1995

. . . the hunter knows not only how to kill the animal, but also how to preserve it and how to respect it so that it will come to the shore next year.

> Petr Typykhkak, Sireniki, February 1996

The spiritual relationship existing between hunters and the animals they hunt, and between women and the food species they prepare for eating, is a deeply personal one. Therefore, some Inuit speak of these strong personal feelings and beliefs as having spiritual significance, whereas to others they may be referred to as their personal, moral, or ethical beliefs. Some years ago, the late

FIGURE 12. Bowhead mattak being shared at Nalukataq festival. Barrow, Alaska, June 1990.

Eben Hopson, founder of the Inuit Circumpolar Conference (ICC) and the Alaska Eskimo Whaling Commission, explicitly linked whaling to religious observance when he stated:

> The whale is more than food to us. It is the centre of our life and culture. We are the People of the Whale. The taking and sharing of the whale is our Eucharist and Passover. The whaling festival is our Easter and Christmas, the Arctic celebration of the mysteries of life.

Other Inuit continue to echo these sentiments that tie the whale to the destiny of people and give profound meaning to the Inuit subsistence quest for food and social continuity in a challenging environment:

> It is the belief of my people that the patterns of our Eskimo way of life are governed by the resources and the environment which the Creator has provided for our survival. . . . The Eskimos believe that the bowhead whale is a gift, and presents itself as a gift from its Creator . . . which leads us to the ceremonies of sharing and giving of the bowhead whale in our culture . . . because the Eskimos believe that the whale belongs not only to the crew who lands the whale, but to all the community as intended by the power that runs life in this world.
>
> *Marie Adams, Barrow, 1982*

This notion of the whale as a gift from a higher power, a gift deserving of respect and with a high degree of autonomy in its relationship with human beings, is commonly expressed:

Sharing and good feelings in camp are important. You won't have successful hunting if people are disagreeing or unfriendly to each other. You must not speak of getting an animal. . . . If they want to give themselves they will, if they don't, you won't have any success.

Dorothy Arey, Aklavik, August 1991

During whaling, everybody is together. In the village, people on the shore look to sea and are waiting, speaking with each other pleasantly. Nobody is swearing—whales don't like people swearing, or being greedy or evil. In that case they travel far away from shore in order to avoid such people.

Petr Typkhkak, Sireniki, February 1996

When I am preparing to go whale hunting . . . I look to God and pray first. . . . When the whale doesn't want to be caught, the hunter cannot catch him.

Otis Ahkivgak, Barrow, September 1977

Whaling is a sacred affair to the Iñupiat hunter. . . . The belief that spirits are embodied in sea mammals is very strong among the northern Inuit. . . . An appropriate ceremony must be conducted when a whale is landed by the whaling crew to avoid insult to the spirit of the whale and other sea mammals.

Herbert O. Anungazuk, Wales, March 1994

If a pregnant female was taken, the foetus was handled as if it was an adult whale: its belly was first cut so as not to offend the spirits.

Albert Ashkamakin, Yanrakynnot, October 1995

Cultural and spiritual ties to the bowhead are very strong for us. . . . After the whale is struck and landed . . . if we have an elder in the vicinity, he will do the prayer for the whale; that's the first thing. And the process goes on where, if we're towing it . . . everyone gets on the CB radio during those hours and keeps the spiritual thing going. . . . We have slightly different systems as to how we treat the bowhead whale in each community, and we respect each community as to how they treat the bowhead whale, spiritually and culturally. . . . As whaling captain Raymond Hawley of Kivalina said, cultural and spiritual ties to the bowhead are very strong for us.

Burton Rexford, Barrow, March 1994

SUGGESTED READINGS

Attungana, P. 1985. Keynote address to the Alaska Eskimo Whaling Captains' Convention, held in Barrow, February 1985. Printed in *Alaska Native News*, June 1985:9–11.

Bodenhorn, B. 1990. "I'm not the great hunter, my wife is." *Etudes/Inuit/Studies* 14:55–74.

Dahl, J. 1989. The integrative and cultural role of hunting and subsistence in Greenland. *Etudes/Inuit/Studies* 13(1):23–42.

Hansen, J. C., H. S. Pedersen, and G. Mulvad. 1994. Fatty acids and antioxidants in the Inuit diet. Their role in Ischemic Heart Disease (IHD) and possible interactions with other dietary factors: A review. *Arctic Medical Research* 53:4–17.

Kapel, F. O., and R. Petersen. 1984. Subsistence hunting—the Greenland case. *Reports of the International Whaling Commission*, Special Issue No. 4:51–73.

Kleivan, I. 1996. An ethnic perspective on Greenlandic food. In: B. Jacobsen (ed.), *Cultural and Social Research in Greenland 95/96: Essays in Honour of Robert Petersen*, pp. 146–57. Nuuk: Ilisimatusarfik/Atuakkiorfik.

Lowenstein, T. 1993. *Ancient Land: Sacred Whale. The Inuit Hunt and Its Rituals*. New York: Farrar, Straus, and Giroux.

Lynge, F. 1992. *Arctic Wars: Animals Rights, Endangered Peoples*. Hanover, NH, and London: University Press of New England.

McCartney, A. P. 1995. *Hunting the Largest Animals: Native Whaling in the Western Arctic and Subarctic*. Studies in Whaling No. 3, Occasional Paper No. 36, Canadian Circumpolar Institute, Edmonton.

Marquardt, O., and R. A. Caulfield. 1996. Development of West Greenlandic markets for country foods since the 18th century. *Arctic* 49(2):107–19.

Rasmussen, K. 1929. *The Intellectual Life of the Iglulik Eskimos*. Report of the Fifth Thule Expedition 1921–24, vol. 7(1):9–304.

Stoker, S. W., and I. I. Krupnik. 1993. Subsistence whaling. In: J. J. Burns, J. J. Montague, and C. J. Cowles (eds.), *The Bowhead Whale*, pp. 579–629. Lawrence, Kans.: The Society for Marine Mammalogy.

Usher, P. J., M. Baikie, Marianne Demmer, D. Nakashima, M. G. Stevenson, and M. Stiles. 1995. *Communicating About Contaminants in Country Food: The Experience of Aboriginal Communities*. Ottawa: Inuit Tapirisat of Canada.

Wenzel, G. 1989. *Animal Rights, Human Rights: Economy, Ecology and Ideology in the Canadian Arctic*. London: Belhaven Press.

CHAPTER TWO

Whaling by Inuit:
Yesterday, Today, and Tomorrow

BELUGA HUNTING

. . . beluga is very important for all of us, because of our culture, how it's used by our grandparents and parents: it is important for food, culture, lifestyle—it is very important to us! . . . . [It is] important to let the world know that conservation and protection of beluga is important for our life as food and for the continuation of our culture.

David Aglukark, Arviat, April 1996

Alaska

Ancestors of Alaska's Inuit people were involved in beluga hunting as early as 5,500 years ago, in the time of the Denbigh people, who are considered to be the ancestors of contemporary Iñupiat. The Denbigh people, like the present-day Inuit, hunted beluga in the early part of the summer. The descendants of these early people also led a migratory existence, visiting the coast in spring and summer especially to take part in collective whale hunts. These drives were seen to be very important, according to a Russian explorer named Zagoskin, who provided the first written account of Alaskan beluga drive hunting in 1840:

The most important beluga hunting . . . takes place with the big drives at Pashtol [Pastol] Bay, where all the coastal people of the south shore of Norton Sound congregate about the middle of July. They choose a quiet day, and when the tide is full, they sail out in 100 or more kayaks to the edge of the deep water. . . . As they move forward in pursuit, the natives keep absolute silence, but when they have gone out to a certain distance, at a signal from one of the old men who has been chosen, they start to make the greatest possible noise: they beat drums, strike their paddles on the kayaks, they do not shout, but bellow, and slowly, carefully, they move in toward the shore as the tide starts to go out. . . . In a good year the hunters may round up as many as a hundred head [of beluga whales] in one drive. During the whole process the people who stayed ashore, young and old, try to observe the strictest possible silence.

During this period in northwest Alaska, beluga were important to Inuit diets, trading practices, identity, and cultural beliefs. Beluga were part of a seasonal cycle of inland/coastal subsistence pursuits that involved the taking of salmon, caribou and other inland game, and marine mammals. Beluga drives undertaken from camps like Sisualik on Kotzebue Sound and Siniq (Elephant Point) on Eschscholtz Bay invigorated and reaffirmed social relations between hunters from different areas in the region. Typically, a drive hunt would be guided by a shaman and led by a distinguished hunter from one Iñupiat nation, assisted by two or more allies from neighbouring nations. In preparation for the hunt, Inuit families followed spiritually based rules and prohibitions so that beluga would give themselves willingly to hunters, and to ensure a safe hunt. Beluga hunting camps were also a place where Inuit were able to gather together with relatives from other areas, and where people traded valued foods and other items among themselves.

An account of beluga hunting in the 1870s, provided by an elder, called Aluniq, describes the high degree of organization and cooperation in a collective beluga drive in Eschscholtz Bay:

They made a line and moved together. They hollered, splashed their paddles, waved their harpoons to scare them into real shallow water. Those belugas always tried to go back to deep water, but hunters chased them back into water that was shallower than two-and-a-half feet. . . . Hunters picked big beluga and chose them first. Every hunter had his own mark on his harpoon. The marks were red and black paint so every hunter knew his own harpoons if he struck a beluga and lost it. . . . When a hunter got a beluga, he ties it to his qayaq [kayak] and brought it to shore; if he get two, he'd tie one on each side. . . . If wind came up while men were out hunting, women would take umiaqs [skin boats] off the racks and go to help those hunters who were towing two belugas. People always helped together when they landed and pulled those beluga on the shore.

Once a beluga was brought on shore, women in the camp would begin butchering and processing the animal. Using the woman's knife (*ulu*), the local women would cut the whale into large pieces that would then be distributed widely to other participants in the hunt and to their families. Anthropologists Lucier and VanStone describe how this was done, based on Aluniq's account:

> Maktak from the front flippers forward was given to widows and those who had no men to hunt. . . . [T]he man who killed a beluga with a spear received half the carcass . . . A youth's first kill was distributed widely to the elderly, whether related or not, so little was left over for the young hunter's household.

In the twentieth century, beluga hunting continues to be important to Inuit families and communities in Alaska, despite significant social and cultural changes. Beluga are used for food and as a source of oil, with the mattak being particularly prized. Today, beluga hunting occurs in about thirty communities extending from Cook Inlet in the south, to Bristol Bay, Norton Sound, the Yukon-Kuskokwim Delta, northwest Alaska, and then east to the Canadian border.

Hunters typically use one of four methods for catching beluga: shooting and harpooning from the ice edge in spring, shooting in open water from boats, netting them, or driving the animals into shallow water. Ice-edge hunting is common during the northward migrations in spring, when whales swim in the narrow leads. As sea ice melts in early summer, hunters begin open-water hunting when beluga are spotted near camps or encountered by chance during other activities. Netting is most common in summer and fall at headlands and at locations where deeper water and a favourable shoreline make this technique productive. Beluga drives, as noted above, are most common in shallow bays and estuaries (such as Point Lay and Wainright).

Each of these methods changed in the late nineteenth and early to mid-twentieth centuries as a result of catastrophic epidemics among the Inuit, the introduction of rifles and powered boats, the imposition of Western schooling, the effects of alcohol, and the suppression of indigenous spiritual practices. Since the late 1940s and early 1950s, beluga hunters have also employed increasingly powerful outboard motors mounted on fibreglass or aluminum skiffs; as these boats draw more water than did the skin boats, some camps located near shallow waters have been abandoned. Although powerful outboard motors enable hunters to approach and pursue beluga, local hunters are also aware that beluga are particularly sensitive to sounds and smells associated with skiffs and gasoline-powered motors.

Hunters observe that in recent years, with the use of larger outboard motors and more boat activity, it has become harder to approach beluga than in earlier years when motors of less than 10 HP were in use. Beluga rarely come close to shore as they used to, and in some areas where commercial fishing takes place and a high degree of boat use occurs, beluga are no longer present. On the approach of a motorized boat, some beluga dive to the bottom and remain motionless until they surface to breathe after about twenty minutes. Hunters claim that the use of CB radios with ultra-high frequency (UHF) transmission also disturbs beluga; in earlier times, keeping quiet was considered very necessary when hunting beluga. When today's elders were young, there were strict rules about keeping quiet while camping at the important beluga hunting areas (for example, Elephant Point in Eschscholtz Bay) and, of course, during the hunt itself.

Despite such changes, beluga hunting—and the products it provides—continues to be practiced and valued by local Inuit. Moreover, in pursuing greater political and economic self-determination, there is growing awareness of the need to revitalize indigenous hunting practices. For example, hunters in Eschscholtz Bay in recent years have sought to reinstate a coordinated drive hunt, with a single drive commander.

The meat is often dried for one to three days and then stored in whale oil. It will also be frozen for later use. Mattak is also stored in oil or frozen. The meat and mattak will be boiled, or, in the case of mattak, also eaten raw. The oil is used to treat sores, frostbite (its use will prevent scarring), and earache.

Canada

Whaling in our Inuit society plays a very important role. Although not all Inuit in this area harvest or choose not to harvest belugas, they know and understand its importance to our people and culture. Our people have traditionally harvested whales in the summer and made caches for the long winters ahead. Today, we harvest whales by different means but for the same purpose. It is a way of life and offers another source of protein through the winters.

Duane Smith and the Inuvik Hunters and Trappers Committee, June 1995

For centuries, beluga have been hunted by Inuit in kayaks throughout the Canadian Arctic and subarctic; often, two or more hunters cooperated in the hunt. Harpoons attached to sealskin floats would be thrown into the whale before it was lanced in the heart by means of a blade attached to the end of the kayak paddle. Once rifles became widely used, the whale would be shot after one or more floats were attached. In some locations (such as Kittegaryuit in the Mackenzie Delta, and Cumberland Sound), kayakers working cooperatively drove schools of beluga ashore where they were killed. Even a single hunter could drive one or two beluga ashore, a method practiced on the Belcher Islands until hunters stopped using kayaks in the 1960s. An elder from the western Canadian Arctic recalled earlier days:

> Late in June people living along the coast moved to the mouth of the river. . . . When the whales arrived . . . the men went out in their kayaks and drove the whales into shallow water until they grounded and they would kill as many as they could tow ashore. They used spears to kill the whales. The hunters had a wooden tube to blow into the whales . . . it made them easier to tow. The meat was dried and some was stored in sealskin containers with rendered whale oil. All of the food they put up was winter food. The head and tail parts of the whale were stored in pits dug into permafrost and covered with logs. . . . When it was cold enough to freeze, the people took all the meat out of the pits and put it on stages built above the ground.
>
> *Bertram Pokiak, Tuktoyaktuk, 1989*

Figure 14. Bowhead being processed at a Hudson's Bay Company whaling station. Pangnirtung, Canada, 1945.

In the eighteenth, nineteenth, and twentieth centuries, Inuit were employed in commercial beluga whale hunts and drives operated by European whalers and traders (such as at Little Whale River in Northern Quebec, and Pangnirtung, Baffin Island). These commercial operations became integrated into the local Inuit economic and social life, as men and women worked in catching and processing the several hundred whales taken each summer. The hunt was principally to obtain blubber and skins, which were shipped to European markets. The Inuit were able to use the meat and some of the mattak, in addition to receiving wages and trade goods, which in a number of cases included wooden whale boats (which allowed Inuit to hunt more effectively).

Beluga are the most commonly and widely taken whale species in Canada, with hunters from Northern Labrador and the coasts of Nunavik (northern Quebec), Hudson Bay, Foxe Basin, the coast of Baffin Island, the south coast of Ellesmere Island, Somerset Island, and along the Beaufort Sea coast and the mouth of the Mackenzie River in the Western Arctic, regularly taking whales during the open water season. Very occasionally, whales will be taken west of Somerset Island in the east-central Canadian Arctic, or during the winter at any of the summering locations, if trapped as the winter ice forms.

Communities in the Hudson Strait and Hudson Bay may take beluga at the floe edge in winter; in Labrador, beluga have been hunted at the floe edge as they migrate north in the spring. In the western Canadian Arctic, hunters take beluga in the summer from whale camps along the Yukon coast, in the shallow bays surrounding the Mackenzie River delta, and eastward beyond the Tuktoyaktuk Peninsula. In some years in this latter area, whales become trapped in Husky Lakes as ice forms in the fall; when local hunters decide the whales are too numerous to survive on the limited food available in these lakes, they may hunt them. On some occasions, hunters from Tuktoyaktuk have driven beluga through a narrow portion of Husky Lakes, and then returned once the ice formed to kill the trapped beluga. To prevent the whales' escape from Husky Lakes, a line of long bones is strung across the narrow passage, the noise from which keeps the whales from approaching the narrows.

Beluga are mostly hunted from skiffs and freighter canoes powered by outboard motors, though larger wooden boats with inboard motors are also used. Nets and drives are now only rarely employed; in the western Canadian Arctic, nets (45 cm mesh) were commonly in use about thirty years ago, though even at that time hunters preferred taking beluga with guns and harpoons from their boats. Netting for whales has occurred at other location (such as Salluit, in Hudson Strait) where migrating whales predictably swim past suitable net-setting locations. The use of sealskin kayaks for hunting beluga ended in the

FIGURE 15. Beluga whales taken at a *sassat* (winter whale trap) in the sea ice. Jones Sound, Canada, March 1967.

1960s, the last kayaks being in use in northern Quebec and on the Belcher Islands in southeast Hudson Bay. Harpoons with detachable heads are commonly used in hunting, as are floats (formerly made from an entire ringed-seal skin, but now from a variety of imported materials) and rifles (from 30.06 down to .222 calibre).

Canadian Inuit value beluga mattak highly, and therefore after a successful hunt it is widely distributed among family members and neighbours. In the Western Arctic whaling camps, the first whale landed will usually be distributed equally to all those present at the camp. Subsequently, the distribution is to members of the successful hunting group participating in that particular hunt, with those receiving the initial shares handling a secondary distribution to families and other community members. In many communities (for instance, Sanikiluaq, in southeast Hudson Bay) a successful hunt is reported on the community radio, with an invitation to all to collect a share, ensuring complete utilization of the carcass. Whereas in many regions in the Eastern Arctic beluga meat has been regarded principally as dog food, Inuit in Nunavik and on the Belcher Islands make complete use of the beluga carcass as food. Beluga meat in some of these communities is divided into portions, some of which are only eaten by men and other portions only by women. Inuit specifically recognize that using beluga in this way helps socialization of the individual by defining gender roles and emphasizing codependency of males and females in society. Beluga hunting is considered to be very important, not just to provide food, but also to enable sharing and exchange among kinfolk to occur. In this region, as elsewhere in the Arctic, Inuit emphasize that if they were not able to hunt and eat local foods they would lose part of their identity.

> We had so many whales in Repulse Bay that we lived on mattak. . . . I would think our people will always hunt whales because it is something we do: it is part of our culture, and I think culturally what you eat is very, very important. Inuit identity is important: Inuit don't get a lot of identity out of eating beef.
> *Michael Kusugak, Rankin Inlet, March 1995*

The mattak is usually eaten fresh and raw, though some now deep-fry it, and others allow it to age before eating it. The flippers and tail flukes are highly prized as food. The posterior sections of the carcass provide the best mattak if it is to be eaten aged. The dried beluga stomach makes a good container for aging beluga mattak and meat. Elders in the Western Arctic report that the mattak cut from the front of the head or along the spine is particularly tasty, and that they also like eating heart and kidneys, either roasted or boiled. They

FIGURE 16. Taking home beluga mattak. Arviat, Canada, July 1988.

also report that an appealing snack food can be prepared from the outer layer of mattak (called *kanniq*) which is either aged or smoked, with the kanniq from female beluga providing the most desirable snack.

Throughout the Eastern Arctic, the meat is usually air-dried before eating. On the Belcher Islands, a sausage is made by placing whale blubber into sections of intestine, which are lightly boiled before being air-dried or smoked; this sausage is often eaten with dried whale meat. In Cumberland Sound, the meat near the ribs and closest to the backbone is favoured by elders, and mattak will be eaten fried as well as eaten raw or in aged condition. The meat and gray-coloured mattak of younger beluga are generally preferred over the meat and mattak of large adult beluga; large male beluga in particular are considered too tough to be enjoyable.

Perhaps because there is always a high demand for mattak, only small amounts are sold for redistribution through retail outlets in the Canadian Arctic. However, some full-time hunters sell portions of their catch to finance their hunting activities, and over the years the various levels of government (including Inuit municipal authorities and hunters' and trappers' associations) have attempted to encourage intersettlement trade so that wage-employed Inuit in the larger towns continue to have access to healthy and culturally appropriate food, and also so that hunters can earn an income.

Beluga oil was considered a superior lamp oil, better than seal oil for softening skins, and used for cleaning and lubricating guns and other equipment. A number of medicinal uses are reported for beluga oil in the Western Arctic, including use as a liniment or ointment for sores and rashes, for ear and eye drops, and as an emetic or purgative (to cause vomiting).

Greenland

The hunting of beluga in Greenland has a long and varied history. For many centuries, hunting satisfied local needs for meat, mattak, blubber, sinew, and food for dogs. However, in colonial times the blubber and oil in particular became an important trade commodity, with the oil being exported to Europe. Thus, in some districts (Maniitsoq in southwest Greenland, for one) large-scale drive fisheries were started by the Greenland Trade Department and continued for several years, until the warming of west Greenland waters in the 1930s caused the beluga to move northward. However, similar commercial drive fisheries occurred for several decades further north in the Upernavik municipality, where beluga remained abundant. However, by the 1950s the European market for whale oil had disappeared, and large-scale drive fisheries ceased operating.

At the beginning of this century, beluga hunting was more extensively pursued along the coast than in recent years, with beluga taken as far south as the Alluitsoq district, in the extreme south of Greenland. Following the warming of the waters off southern Greenland and the disappearance of beluga, the younger people became unfamiliar with mattak as an item of diet; however, older people and those who had moved to the southern districts from farther north wished to continue eating mattak. Thus, in the 1950s, with improvements in coastal communications and refrigeration then available in the communities, the market for mattak spread back into the former whaling districts in southern Greenland.

As a consequence of these new markets, in the 1960s the Greenland Trade Department once again resumed purchasing mattak in the northern hunting districts and reselling it along the coast. Due to the variability in catches, and hence an unsatisfied demand at some times and places, the price began to rise and beluga (as well as narwhal) hunting allowed hunters' incomes to improve. In an effort to increase catches, hunters in the Upernavik district at the end of the 1960s had reinstated a drive fishery for beluga, using skiffs driven by outboard motors. The success of this drive fishery resulted in a local by-law that stated that after a particular day in September, the only beluga hunts allowed were collective drive fisheries. A drive fishery is also practiced in the Disko Bay region.

The hunting season for beluga extends from October or November until June from Aasiaat north to Disko Bay, and from April through November from Uummannaq and to the north. Until the 1920s, beluga appeared in the fiords near Nuuk during the winter months and were hunted until the spring when they left the region on their northward migration. Beluga are hunted from skiffs from the northern districts south to Sisimiut, with hunting from cutters practiced from Upernavik to Maniitsoq district in the south. Beluga are only allowed to be taken by boats of less than 25 gross tonnage, and although larger fishing vessels can take these whales for use by the crew on board, the crew is not allowed to sell whale products. Kayaks are used in the northern districts. Netting and ice-edge hunting takes place from Upernavik south to Ilulissat. Beluga are only rarely taken in East Greenland. Rifles used in these hunts are typically 30.06 or 7.62 mm calibre, with the heavier 375 Magnum sometimes used in floe-edge hunting.

Beluga are ordinarily hunted from kayaks and motorized skiffs and similar small boats, often by single boats or pairs of hunters, but sometimes cooperatively when a larger number of small boats captures small numbers of beluga swimming together. In the latter case, an equal distribution of meat and mattak takes place among the participants in the hunt after the whales are cut up on shore. The edible products will be further distributed throughout the community by various means, including being sold at the local market. Beluga mattak remains a highly desired food, and can always be disposed of within the family and through local trade outlets. It has become a tradition in Greenland to serve mattak (often from beluga) at any official, or special public or private, functions.

Russia

Beluga hunting in Chukotka occurs in several villages, though the numbers taken are small due to the customary use of larger whales and walrus. Moreover, while beluga are common, they move quickly from place to place along the coast, occurring at any location for a short time only; beluga consequently contribute only in limited ways to the local economy and diet. The arrival, presence, and departure of beluga appear to coincide with the appearance of migratory fish (principally arctic char or arctic cod) in the coastal areas, such that in some years, beluga occur during winter months—they can break ice up to 15 cm thick—as fish move into the bays and coastal waters.

Beluga hunting occurs either from shore, at the edge of the sea ice (as in the New Chaplino region) or both at the ice edge and from boats (as at Sireniki). Hunters hide behind ice hummocks and shoot the whale using a 9 mm or 7.62 mm (rarely 5.6 mm) rifle when the whale is about 25–30 metres from the ice edge; a floating grappling hook on a line is used to retrieve the dead whale. In some cases, if the water is not too deep, the dead whale will be hooked from a small boat. If hunting occurs at the ice edge, in most cases the whale is pulled onto the ice for butchering, but if this is not possible it will be cut up in the water. A pulley system may be used to drag the whale from the water, using a bone or steel pin set in the ice. Hunting from boats is rare today, owing to the speed with which beluga swim away from the sound of the motors. In earlier times, when sailing boats were in use, it was possible to hunt beluga from boats in open water; at those times silence was strictly observed, and hunters were not allowed to move around on the boats during hunting.

Almost all parts of the beluga are used for food. The meat is dried, and also eaten frozen, boiled, or fried. The mattak is eaten raw, fresh, boiled, or fried. The liver and kidneys are eaten boiled or fried. The stomach and intestines may be boiled with meat, and the brain, tongue, tail flukes, and flippers are also boiled; the heart is eaten after being lightly boiled with blood, or it may be lightly fried. Lungs may be dried and eaten with fat, or eaten frozen. The mattak, flukes, and flippers may be aged before being eaten. Beluga oil is used with fish and salad plants, and also for medicinal purposes: it is effective in the treatment of frostbite and gastric ulcers. Although in the past beluga oil was traded for reindeer meat and skins, in recent years the oil has been sold to the village fur farms. Unless the oil is mixed with other foods, it is not considered suitable for dog food. The skin is used to make boot soles (which tend not to slip), belts, and lines, though it is mainly used when bearded-seal and walrus hide is not available. Beluga sinew is sometimes used to sew walrus-skin boat covers.

BOWHEAD HUNTING

The time is almost here,
The season of the deep blue sea . . .
Bringing good things from the deep blue sea.
Whale of a distant ocean . . .
May there be a whale.
May it indeed come . . .
Inside the waves.
—*St. Lawrence Island prayer song, Alaska*

It is likely the elaborate organization for successful bowhead whaling developed in the Bering Strait region about 2,000 years ago, with the use of large skin-covered boats, toggling harpoons, large lances, and slate and stone flensing knives. It seems likely that these technologies were sufficiently developed so that by about 1,000 years ago, hunting bowhead whales was proficient enough to assist the Inuit of the day to expand into the Canadian Arctic and into Greenland at a time when the climate was favourable to the presence of bowhead whales throughout the Arctic. The hunt was usually collaborative, with several boats approaching the slow-swimming bowhead and the harpoons with floats being used to tire the whale, which was then killed using a four-metre long lance tipped with stone or bone. The harpoons were about two metres in length with a bone or ivory foreshaft fitted with a detachable toggling head made of slate or, sometimes, iron. It is believed that this traditional hunt resulted in about forty-five to sixty bowhead being taken each year by Iñupiat along the Alaskan coast east of the Bering Strait.

These customary whaling practices changed starting in the 1850s, when American commercial whalers followed the bowhead whales north of the

Bering Strait. As many as 200 commercial whaling vessels were soon whaling along the northern Alaskan coast, and shore stations were set up at several Iñupiat whaling villages, such as at Kingigin (Wales), Tikigaq (Point Hope), and Utqiagvik (Barrow). The Iñupiat were employed as crew members, harpooners, flensers (who cut up the whale carcasses), and general workers at the shore stations; access to modern technology, including wooden whaleboats, hand-held explosive-grenade whaling lances and guns, and metal tools, resulted in the traditional whaling technology's being put aside. Working for wages, engaging in trade for rifles, iron tools and utensils, cloth, and a variety of imported foods and tobacco, created a variety of dependencies on the whaler-traders, including movement of people to areas where the whalers set up shore stations and trading posts.

Despite these technological, dietary, and economic changes, the Iñupiat maintained many other elements of their traditional whaling culture. Thus, in 1890, there were 400 Iñupiat whaling at Barrow, using seventy skin-covered *umiat* and ten wooden whaleboats, sharing whale products and engaging in the traditional whaling ceremonies. By 1910, most commercial whaling ended due to the collapse of southern markets for whalebone (baleen) and whale oil. As the commercial whaler-traders withdrew from the Arctic, Alaskan Yup'iit and Iñupiat in seventeen communities resumed bowhead hunting at levels approximating those existing before the commercial whalers entered the Arctic almost sixty years earlier.

Bowhead whaling takes place today in ten villages: two Yup'iit communities (St. Lawrence Island), and eight Iñupiat villages extending from Wales to Kaktovik near to the Alaska–Canada border and on Little Diomede Island in the Bering Sea. Before the hunt begins, whalers usually take their harpoons, grenades, and floats to the church where they are blessed, and the congregation prays for a safe and successful hunt.

Most bowhead hunting takes place in the spring, when bowhead migrate north through the Bering Strait and move to summer feeding areas in the Canadian Beaufort Sea. During this spring migration, whaling takes place during the few weeks beginning in early April when the land-fast ice remains safe enough to hunt from skin-covered boats as the bowheads move eastward in open water leads at the edge of the ice.

Hand-held weapons, based on the whaling technology introduced by American commercial whalers in the 1880s, are still used to kill bowheads. These weapons include the darting gun, used to attach a line and float to the whale as well as firing an explosive grenade deep into the whale's body. A smooth-bore shoulder gun, firing an explosive grenade, is used as a secondary

FIGURE 17. Spring hunting for bowhead at the floe edge. Barrow, Alaska, May 1990.

killing weapon. In the spring hunts, the whales are towed to the ice edge and normally pulled onto the ice by means of a block and tackle system, but if ice conditions prevent this, the carcass may be cut up in the water. Nearby crews may cooperate in both hunting and cutting up the carcass. Shares are widely and equitably distributed, and in most communities, virtually every household receives its share from every whale that is taken. Community members living outside the community will also receive shares, especially of mattak.

Sharing bowhead meat and mattak continues outside of the whaling season, for whaling captains set aside part of their catch for various whaling festivals. These festivals include the Whale's Tail feasts, *Aniruq* and *Qinu* (held in spring or fall, respectively), and *Qagruq* or *Nalukataq* held in June (at Point Hope and Kivalina), *Apugauti* and *Nalukataq* (the major whaling festival at the end of spring whaling in Barrow, Wainright, and Nuiqsut), and on Thanksgiving Day and at Christmas (in every Alaskan whaling community). Ice cellars in the permafrost, as well as electric freezers, are used for storing the meat and mattak, and when the meat is brought out of storage at these festivals, everyone receives a share; as one Point Hope elder noted: *"Whether they are a mean person or a good person, it doesn't matter. It's a time of giving."*

Two Iñupiat communities furthest to the east (Nuiqsut and Kaktovik) have no spring whaling season; here bowhead are hunted in October as the whales migrate westward after spending the summer in Canadian waters. The community of Barrow has both a fall open-water bowhead hunt as well as a spring ice-edge hunt.

These open-water hunts in the fall use fibreglass or metal boats powered by outboard engines. In the case of St. Lawrence Island, where open-water hunts also take place in spring and summer, skin-covered boats will be sailed, paddled, or powered by outboard motors (which are especially important when towing the whale back to the community). The same darting guns, floats, and shoulder guns are used at every season. In the case of fall hunts, the whales are towed to shore near to the community, where they can be pulled on land using a tractor or truck. The same community-wide distribution of meat and mattak takes place at the time the whale is cut up, with a further distribution occurring during the fall and winter whaling festivals.

The hunting technology in use today is undergoing further development: the grenades are being improved to increase hunter safety and killing effectiveness. Thus the black powder charge in the grenade is now being replaced by a penthrite charge, with safety improvements made to the firing mechanism. Further changes include attaching a radio transmitter to the float so that harpooned whales can more readily be followed during open-water hunts conducted when visibility is poor.

Canada

> There is plenty of meat on a bowhead whale, and all parts were used by our ancestors . . . the bones, meat, blubber, and other parts. It is evident that bowheads did have ties to the Inuit traditional way of life. . . . Our ancestors had uses for every part of the bowhead—and I'm sure we could adopt their uses.
> *Takealook Temela, Lake Harbour, April 1995*

The archaeological record indicates that various species of whales have been hunted in northern regions of Canada for at least 2,000 years. From about A.D. 1100 to 1400 the ancestors of today's eastern Canadian Arctic Inuit hunted bowhead whales (as well as beluga and narwhal). Bowhead hunting became restricted as the climate cooled (during the "Little Ice Age") and the sea remained ice-choked for most of the year; however, whaling continued in some favourable localities (such as Cumberland Sound, and in northern Labrador).

FIGURE 18. Drummers performing during Nalukataq festival. Barrow, Alaska, June 1990.

In the early 1800s, whaling ships from European nations entered Lancaster Sound in search of bowhead whales. By the 1840s, the British were whaling in Cumberland Sound, where whalers noted that the local Inuit customarily made annual catches of eight to twelve bowhead. In the 1860s, British and American whalers also entered Hudson Bay. In both localities, Inuit were hired to crew the wooden whaleboats, to work as flensers, and to transport baleen and blubber by dog sled from the ice edge. When not engaged in whaling, Inuit men hunted for fresh food and Inuit women manufactured arctic clothing for the whalers.

The most prized items the Inuit obtained from the whalers were wooden whaleboats, rifles, and telescopes. While rifles tended to individualize hunting, the ownership of wooden boats reinforced the authority of the outstanding leaders and whaler-hunters among the Inuit, and hence strengthened preexisting camp social arrangements. Thus, commercial whaling became firmly embedded in the Inuit lifestyle and culture, especially in northwest Hudson Bay and in Cumberland Sound. However, the depletion of whales in the eastern Canadian Arctic, together with the introduction of cheaper and easily available substitutes for whale oil and baleen in southern markets, resulted in fewer whaling ships arriving each spring from Europe and New England. Thus, after about 1870, a progressively greater reliance was placed by the shore-based whaling stations on Inuit whaling crews to continue supplying them with bowhead baleen and blubber. The final collapse of these commercial operations, in both

FIGURE 19. Inuit commercial bowhead whalers. Southampton Island, Canada, 1903. [Public Archives of Canada/C 46972]

the Eastern and Western Arctic regions, followed from the discovery of abundant petroleum-based substitutes for whale oil in the second decade of this century. For Inuit, who had become accustomed to the now-familiar pattern of living near the whaling stations, the eventual closing of the whaling stations brought about real hardship and a sense of melancholy: *"Everybody had things to do and no-one questioned their responsibilities,"* remembered Etuangat Aksayook of Pangnirtung, who in 1984 looked back on those days fondly.

The pursuit of bowhead whales by hunters in kayaks, and in some regions also utilizing skin-covered multipurpose boats (*umiat*), continued into recent historic times, and though the European and American commercial whalers introduced new whaling technology during the nineteenth century, a vigorous oral tradition has kept alive in people's memories the more traditional ways of hunting whales. The customary hunting technique consisted of hunters in kayaks pursuing, and tiring, the whale so that it remained on the surface and could be more easily lanced. Whether hunting from *umiat* or from wooden boats, the whale was approached from the rear and to one side, with the harpooner thrusting several harpoons with attached lines, floats, and often a large drag anchor into the whale. Once guns became available, shots were fired at the whale, forcing it to dive frequently and thus further tiring it; Inuit say that gunfire forces the whale to tense its muscles, thus oxygenating the blood and helping keep the animal afloat. When the whale could no longer submerge at all, the steersman thrust a long lance into the heart, killing the whale almost instantly.

At some eastern arctic localities, hunting was carried out by hunters in kayaks alone. This technique entailed a large number of hunters paddling up to the bowhead and repeatedly lancing it in the kidney region with a blade attached to the end of their kayak paddles. This was done quietly, one hunter at a time making an attack without alarming the whale, so that after a period of hours the whale died through loss of blood without fleeing from the hunters.

A man in a kayak . . . is no threat to a whale. The kayak is silent, moves quickly and is much better to handle than any umiaq. . . . When we saw whales we could move among them and they were not afraid of our little kayaks. There was no fear of trying to kill a great whale if you know how to do it. My father was such a man. He was the one who knew the right place to stick in the spear. He would paddle beside the whale, carefully looking at her body. There is a place below her spine where you can see a movement. . . . That's where the kidney is, and that's the only place where it is safe to stick the spear. This was done carefully and quietly, and you may be surprised to know that the whale did not even know that she was being killed. There was no fight. She kept swimming on. . . . We would follow her sometimes for a very long time until she died.

Jim Kilabuk, Pangnirtung, 1985

In the western Canadian Arctic, two of the five Mackenzie Inuit subgroups traditionally hunted the bowhead whale by sending out parties of hunters in kayaks; these Inuit killed a small number of whales each summer. However, it is thought that bowhead did not contribute importantly to these people's economies, though oral tradition preserves the identity of famous local hunters: Niolomaluk, Kikniktak, and Napiguk are three such renowned men. Among these Inuit, it was the practice to tattoo successful hunters from the mouth to the ears each time they killed a bowhead: one man, Nowyavuk, had three such tattoos, it is recalled. A Western Arctic elder recalls bowhead whaling:

> Further east of Tuktoyaktuk, along the coast where the water is deeper, people used skin boats to hunt bowhead. . . . They used spears with barbs, long lines and avatuks [skin floats]. In about the centre of the line they used a disc about the size of a dinner plate to slow down the speared whale until it was too tired, then it was killed and towed ashore. Nuvogauk [Atkinson Point] . . . was the central place to hunt bowhead whales. The deep water there is right close to shore.

Bertram Pokiak, Tuktoyaktuk, 1989

Contact with American commercial whalers in this area during the late nineteenth and early twentieth centuries resulted in many deaths among the Mackenzie Inuit from introduced diseases. Indeed, it is estimated that more than 90 percent of the Mackenzie Inuit died in the first few years of contact with whalers. However, the whaling tradition was remembered by those surviving, and was reinforced by Iñupiat from Alaska who migrated into the Mackenzie region in the years between the start of World War I until the start of World War II.

The small amount of bowhead whaling in the Canadian Arctic since commercial whaling ended around the start of World War I was initially attributed to the small numbers of whales encountered and, in later years, was a result of active discouragement by Canadian government authorities. However, the evidence now indicates that significant recovery of the bowhead is occurring in the Eastern Arctic:

> . . . right now the numbers are increasing. Back when I was a young lad, when bowhead whale was no longer allowed to be hunted, I was one of the

people who would see a small number of bowhead whales. . . . We can see large groups of bowhead anywhere nowadays. So therefore I think that the bowhead whale population has increased quite a bit since I was a young lad.

Nauya Tassuat, Clyde River, 1995

. . . on occasion we see bowhead whales at the floe edge during the month of May and June between Baffin Island and Igloolik. . . . On the other hand, before that time, you wouldn't dream of ever seeing a bowhead whale at the floe edge.

Simon Iyyriak, Igloolik, 1995

As a young man to the time I married, I only saw very few bowhead whales. As a young man there are places I had never seen a bowhead whale, but today I see bowhead whales at those very same places.

Apak Qaqqasiq, Pangnirtung, 1995

With bowhead more abundant in both eastern and western Canadian Arctic waters in recent years, and with the Inuit right to hunt for subsistence now legally and constitutionally protected in Canada, bowheads are once again being hunted on a regular, though strictly limited, basis. In the western Canadian Arctic, efforts were made to resume bowhead hunting in the 1960s, but it was not until 1991 that the first successful bowhead hunt was carried out by the Inuvialuit. The 1991 hunt involved hunting crews from the community of Aklavik, though the landing, cutting up, distributing, consuming, and celebrating the hunt brought in people from several neighbouring communities. The hunt in 1991, and again in 1996, took place from a summer whaling camp several hours' boat travel from the nearest village. Two boats, powered by outboard engines, each with a three-man crew, undertake the hunt, with safety boats also in the vicinity to offer assistance if needed. The darting guns, floats, and shoulder guns are similar to those used in the Alaskan bowhead hunts. Regionwide distribution of meat and mattak involves all six Inuvialuit communities, as well as other neighbouring aboriginal communities with links to the Inuvialuit through marriage and other alliances. Celebrations are held at the whaling camp following the successful hunt, and also at a community feast and drum dance held in Aklavik.

Inuit in the eastern Canadian Arctic have only occasionally hunted bowhead, since the animals became quite scarce in the early years of the present century. These periodic open-water hunts utilize heavy-bore rifles to kill the whales after a sufficient number of floats have been attached by harpoons. Following the most recent hunts during the summers of 1994 and 1996, the mattak

FIGURE 20. Drum dance to celebrate a successful bowhead hunt. Aklavik, September 1991.

was widely distributed throughout the Eastern Arctic, and in the case of the 1996 hunt, Inuit and Inuvialuit traveled to the site of the successful hunt to participate in the post-hunt celebrations.

Russia

> I now go to the Island to take part in hunting the bowhead whale. The time of this hunt is the best time of life—you respect yourself and respect nature. I dream of living to take part in hunting the bowhead whale here in Sireniki.
> *Petr Typykhkak, Sireniki, July 1994*

It appears that bowhead whaling has ancient origins in the Chukotka region, appearing about 2,000 years ago. The monumentally impressive "Whale Alley" on a small islet off the coast of the Chukchi Peninsula dates from about 400 to 600 years ago and consists of 50 or 60 bowhead whale skulls extending about 600 metres in a geometric pattern. The bones are associated with more than 100 stone-lined pits and other stone structures, all of which attest to the significance of bowhead in the ritual, social, and economic life of the marine-mammal hunters of the day—the ancestors of today's Yup'iit marine hunters.

The seasonal food supplies of the Siberian Yup'iit, in historic times, were always heavily dependent on hunting marine mammals. Whales contributed significantly to the economy of the region because of the proximity of several villages to the migration route of the bowhead and gray whales as they were funneled through the Bering Strait and continued westward along the Chukotkan coast. Thus, open-water hunting of bowhead occurred in October and November as the animals migrated southward, and—with less certainty of success—in the spring on their northward migration.

At the beginning of the twentieth century, with the bowhead population severely reduced by the activities of American commercial whaling operations, Chukotkan native whalers rarely killed more than about a dozen bowheads each year, along with a smaller number of gray whales. In a typical year, two or three bowhead were taken by hunters from Sireniki and Imtuk, one or two from Naukan and Chaplino, and in some years only a single whale by hunters from Avan and Kivak. These hunts utilized the darting and shoulder-gun technology obtained from the American commercial whalers late in the nineteenth century. Each year saw a slight resurgence in bowhead whaling until, in the late 1960s, shore-based whaling by local hunters was stopped by order of the Soviet authorities. At that time, state-organized whaling using a modern catcher boat was introduced, focusing principally on gray whales.

With cessation of bowhead hunting, the Yup'iit obtained their meat and mattak from the gray whale, though this substitution presented the communities with a major cultural problem:

> Hunters are still living today who saw traditional whaling in Chukotka. It will be remembered that their ancestors traditionally harvested the bowhead whale rather than the gray whale (until recently) taken by the catcher boat for residents of the native villages of [Chukotka]. . . . Whaling declines not only every year but every day. That is why the retention and revival of the traditional harvest of the bowhead whale is vital for the majority of the indigenous people of Chukotka.
>
> *Alexander Omrypkir, Anadyr, May 1995*

> For the Eskimos of the Sireniki village, the only true prey is the bowhead whale. Many of us, despite famine, have never tasted the bowhead whale meat. . . . Our whaling ceremonies are devoted to the bowhead whale only. The hunting of this whale, the festivals and rituals in its honour, unite the Eskimos of Chukotka and the [Saint Lawrence] Island.
>
> *Timofei Panaugye, Sireniki, February 1995*

At the present time, the marine-mammal hunters in the Chukotka region are endeavouring to reestablish bowhead whale hunts. This, as Timofei Panaugye points out, is to allow exercise of cultural traditions, which the Yup'iit feel are slipping from their lives at a time of extreme economic and social depression. It is through the reinstatement of bowhead whaling on a regular basis that Chukotkan Yup'iit seek to strengthen their cultural identity, self-sufficiency, and hence self-respect at this time of extreme social, emotional, and physical distress.

Through a cooperative agreement with the Alaskan whalers from the 1998 whaling season onward, the bowhead quota is to be shared. The bowhead quota obtained from the IWC for the years 1998 through 2002 is 280 bowhead, of which the Chukotkans will be allowed five each year.

ASSOCIATION OF INDIGENOUS MINORITIES
OF THE NORTH AND FAR EAST OF THE RUSSIAN FEDERATION

Ul. Stroitelei 8, k. 2, 117876, Moscow, tel. (095) 930-7078
2.04.1996

Dear Alexander Kharlampievich,

There is a disastrous situation connected with providing the indigenous population in Chukotka with food. There is a vicious circle whereby the indigenous population has no means of existence and no means of earning a living. On a number of farms people do not get their wages for more than a year, due to decreased production and problems associated with marketing of the products like meat, fur, fat of marine mammals, etc., and prices for imported foods in rural stores are constantly increasing, thus making these foods virtually inaccessible. This causes suffering, particularly of children, which threatens irreversible consequences regarding survival and the gene pool of the indigenous people.

Under these critical conditions, the indigenous minorities have only one way of survival: by going back to traditional subsistence foodstuffs obtained from the biological resources of the territory.

But that objective cannot be implemented because of the artificial handicaps that impede development of the traditional economies of the peoples of the North. The problem concerns the restoration of a quota for the bowhead whale, the traditional food item of coastal Chukchi and Eskimos. The efforts of indigenous people and the administration of the autonomous Okrug in the solution of this problem has not been successful.

For solving these problems, we wish to request you, Alexander Kharlampievich:

(1) to instruct the Russian delegation to the International Whaling Commission to obtain a quota for five bowhead whales for the indigenous people of Chukotka.

Studies over the last few years, particularly those involving the indigenous population of Chukotka, have demonstrated that the stock has recovered, and is now at a healthy level. Moreover, the hypothesis that Russia has a migratory population of its own bowhead in the Chukchi Sea, the Bering Sea, and the Eastern Siberian Sea, which is not connected with the Alaska population of bowhead whale, is being increasingly supported scientifically.

(2) To allocate special funds for the investigation of the Alaska population of the bowhead whale beginning 1996, because neither Minpriroda RF (Ministry of the Environment), nor Roskomrybolovstvo RF (State Committee for Fisheries) assign funds for conducting such research. The studies should directly involve the indigenous population of Chukotka itself.

This work could be done by research units of Chukotka: Laboratories of Traditional Subsistence of the Research Center "Chukotka," Far Eastern Division; Russian Academy of Sciences and Laboratory of Marine Mammals, Chukchi Division; Pacific Institute of Fisheries and Oceanography, jointly with the organizations of indigenous peoples of Chukotka Nauka; the methods are known and the scientific equipment is available.

(3) The gray whale quota for the Russian Federation should by no means be reduced because this would risk unpredictable consequences for the future of Chukotka and, primarily, the indigenous population.

There is no reason for lowering of the quota, and furthermore, any bargaining regarding the quotas for the indigenous harvest cannot be justified.

(4) We propose that a program of state support for the harvesting, processing, and utilization of the products of indigenous whaling and harvesting of small marine pinnipeds be urgently developed.

Such a program should be comprehensive, including the provision of special weapons, boats, and equipment for the traditional hunt, support for the intensive processing and utilization of the main products and byproducts, including meat, bones, skins, biologically active agents, etc. To accelerate the resolution of these issues, we deem it necessary to purchase special weapons, equipment, and ammunition abroad, where all these are available.

Environmental organizations in a number of countries will take advantage of the imperfections in the traditional harvest and processing of whales in Chukotka; consequently, they will complain about the quotas for indigenous hunt.

(5) To officially nominate a representative of the indigenous peoples of Chukotka to the delegation of the Russian Federation attending the International Whaling Commission, in order to represent and advocate the interests of indigenous hunting in the Russian Federation.

Today, this representative would be proposed by the Association of Indigenous Minorities of Chukotka; however, in future, we intend to establish a Union of Marine Hunters of Russia, which would professionally deal with the problems of marine mammal harvest.

We hope we shall be able to reach mutual understanding.

Sincerely yours,

V.M. Etylin

Vice President
Association of Indigenous Peoples of the North, Siberia and Far East
Russian Federation

GRAY WHALE HUNTING

The importance of whaling for [indigenous peoples] of the coastal zone . . . of Chukotka cannot be overestimated, because whaling for the coastal dwellers of Chukotka is one of the most important elements of their mode of life, with its set of ethical and nutritional components in the life of marine hunters.

Alexander Omrypkir, Anadyr, May 1995

Russia

The gray whale is not only an important source of food and income for the residents of Chukotkan coastal communities, but it also remains an essential part of the local marine-mammal hunting culture. However, these cultural traditions began to be lost when, in 1954, the Soviet authorities banned the hunting of large whales by local hunters using their own traditional boats and weapons, and in its place introduced state-run whaling from the whale catcher-boat *Zvyozdnyi*. The meat from the whales delivered to each community by the catcher-boat was sold, rather than freely shared in the village.

Native residents of Sireniki and Lorino villages have long indicated a desire that the traditional shore-based hunting of both gray and bowhead whales should be revived, though in some villages residents appeared to have been satisfied with the delivery of gray whale carcasses by the annual catcher-boat operation:

In the 1960s–1970s, the killed whales were transported to native villages by the whale catcher-boat *Zvyozdnyi*. The delivery was regular, and the people regularly consumed whale meat. In addition, that practice ensured stable wages, providing work for many village residents, such as melting the fat, cutting up the meat, and doing fur-farm jobs. The animals had food, the fur farm flourished and so did the families of fur farmers.

Lyobov Piskunova, Lorino, April 1995

However, the majority of those interviewed also believed that the revival of shore-based whaling is important for hunters' self-esteem, because hunters' social status in the state farm system of the day was very low. Other reasons for favouring a revival of whale hunting included keeping young people involved in the activity, and the preservation of traditional festivals and rituals associated with whaling that serve to link villages to each other and to their local environment:

The preservation of whaling knowledge, the teaching of children the skills of whaling and associated traditional knowledge, all of which are vital for the revival of the traditional mode of life, for national identity, and for harmonizing the life of the indigenous residents of Chukotka with their environment. . . . The knowledge of whales and whaling is necessary for all residents of Chukotka.

Alexander Omrypkir, Anadyr, May 1995

The last year the *Zvyozdnyi* landed whales was 1992, after which it became imperative that the villages of eastern Chukotka undertake a revival of community-based whaling. That was a very hard time in the coastal communities, for the state farm system had been completely disrupted and workers' wages were (and still are) delayed for half a year and more.

Today the fur farm is declining—half the workers have been laid off, the animal numbers are decreasing and there is no animal food available. . . . There was a period in 1992–1993 when the whaling ship stopped serving us, and our hunters did not resume whaling; a sense of hopelessness prevailed in the village and nobody saw a way out. Today, the hunters have started to harvest whales, but they only kill a few. But that was not bad—everybody tried to get meat for the winter—for they would cut off pieces of meat and mattak to take home.

Lyubov Piskunova, Lorino, April 1995

Thus, in several Chukchi Peninsula villages, gray-whale hunting was resumed. However, the lack of equipment, knowledge, and experience of this form of whaling had serious consequences. Three hunters from Nunlingran died in hunting accidents, and one whaleboat from Sireniki was sunk. But despite the tragic accidents, the residents of all the villages were unanimous in hoping that traditional whaling would be resumed, because they believed that they could not survive without whales. Thus, despite another tragedy involving the death of hunters from Nunlingran in 1994, hunters from seven villages landed fifty-one whales that year.

These hunters' deaths made it apparent that the old whaling traditions had been partly forgotten and that there was a need to revive them. However, many villages did not have elders who knew the methods well enough to teach the young hunters. The most fortunate village in that respect was Lorino, where there were still a number of experienced marine-mammal hunters, who in a short time were able to train young hunters in the rules of whaling, including the correct use of spears, harpoons, and rifles. The hunters of Lorino landed thirty-eight gray whales in 1994.

In 1994, all the villages of the Provideniya region attempted to hunt gray whales out of pressing economic and dietary needs. Sometimes hunters were able to take advantage of events that occur quite often in nature: hunters from both Enmelen and Nunlingran each succeeded in killing gray whales that had already been harassed by killer whales. After these whales were butchered, the meat was utilized by the villagers, with both meat and mattak handed out free of charge. At Sireniki, on the other hand, the meat and mattak of the single whale taken was sold in the community, and the money paid to the hunters.

The spontaneous and rapid revival of gray-whale hunting by village crews had immediate effects. For example, people started recalling what they seemed to have long forgotten: traditional methods of hunting, local ecological knowledge, whaling rituals, and rules of hunter behaviour, including the importance of mutual assistance and sharing between villages. Thus, the revival of traditional whaling acted as a catalyst, noticeably accelerating developments that were hardly detectable in these communities during the Soviet period.

Hunters at Yanrakynnot had neither weapons nor any experience in hunting gray whales, so they requested help from the village of Lorino, about 60 km to the north. Using a skin boat (*baidara*) and a wooden whaleboat sent from Lorino, two gray whales were killed using 7.62 mm rifles and harpoon-spears with wooden shafts and metal heads. The harpoon-spear, with a line and small float attached, is a special whaling implement traditionally used in this region, and still manufactured locally today. Each whaleboat carries seven to ten of the metal harpoon-spears; only one to three wooden shafts are carried, for as the shaft detaches from the metal head, it is then picked up and quickly fitted with a new harpoon head. The harpoon-spear is thrust into the whale's back, in order to hit the main blood vessels, liver, and other vital organs. Such harpoons were formerly used in many villages. This form of hunting is dangerous, so it is usual to have two boats involved for reasons of safety. This method of hunting gray whales is being used in the Provideniya region, where only a few of the oldest hunters remember the whaling traditions. The hunters, for their own safety, try to take smaller or medium-sized whales, as they relearn and teach each other the traditions and techniques needed to sustain their economy, culture, society, and health under difficult and deteriorating living conditions:

> Yes, [whaling is] very important, particularly for the nutrition of indigenous people. We have not been paid our wages for half a year, and we cannot afford to buy imported goods. That is why we rely on marine mammal meat for food. In addition, we sell the meat to the fur farm and are paid in accordance with the weight. The more meat we obtain, the more money we get. . . . It is

FIGURE 21. Flensing a gray whale. Sireniki, Chukotka, 1980.

profitable for us to harvest whales for numerous reasons. . . . I think that in the future the role of the whale harvest will not decline, because it is hardly conceivable that national reforms will assist the life of northern people. Hence, our families will continue to be supported by what we kill. During recent years we revived some traditions and learned to whale from whaleboats, and this is great because whaling is part of our culture.

Sergei Penetegin, Lorino, May 1995

However, at the present time, the Alaskan whalers are assisting the Chukotkan whalers to improve the efficiency and safety of their gray-whale hunts by providing whaling equipment similar to that used in the Alaskan bowhead hunts. As the Chukotkan gray-whale hunt is being enabled to increase toward the number allowed under the International Whaling Commission quota, the IWC decided to reduce the annual quota for the Chukotkan whalers from 140 per year to 120 per year for the years 1998 to 2002.

Thus, gray-whale hunting, which has always been important in the economy of Chukotkan native communities, continues supplying meat, blubber, and mattak, which is eaten frozen, thawed and raw, or boiled. Oil from the blubber is used as food by itself, or added to edible roots, willow leaves, and various sorrels. On rare occasions, humpback whales are also taken.

. . . whaling should be developed today and preserved for the future. Human life continues to heavily depend on whales and marine hunting as a whole. Otherwise, we shall have nothing to live on, nowhere to work, and we shall lose our identity as indigenous people. When a man changes his trade, cut off from his traditions, when he, for example, finds himself a job as a boilerman, he continues to exist as a physical entity but he disappears as a representative of his people. . . . So whaling is essential to the preservation of the traditional culture—if we continue to whale, flense, sew, and process the products, we shall retain our uniqueness.

Lyubov Piskunova, Lorino, April 1995

HUMPBACK AND FIN WHALE HUNTING

Greenland

The large and slow-swimming whales, such as humpback and bowhead, are known to have been hunted in Greenland from skin-covered boats for many centuries. Hunting the faster-swimming fin whales became possible once the

Danish colonial administration introduced a motorized catcher-boat in the 1920s. In addition to the precolonial hunts, Greenlanders were employed in Danish land-based whaling operations run by the colonial administration beginning in 1774 and continuing until 1851. When this whaling ceased, largely as a result of the depletion of bowhead by foreign commercial-whaling fleets operating in Greenlandic and Canadian waters, Greenlanders continued whaling for humpback up until the 1980s.

Due to changing sea ice conditions and attendant food shortages starting in the 1920s, the Danish authorities introduced whale catching from the *Sonja*, a steel catcher-boat of 127 tonnes with a Danish crew, which operated between 1924 and 1949. This vessel could catch larger and fast-swimming whales; for example, in 1927 it landed twenty-two fin whales, nine humpbacks, seven blue whales, and two sperm whales. Thus, west coast communities continued enjoying their customary healthy diet of marine-mammal meat during a period when scarcity of seals in many hunting districts represented a severe threat to people's health and economic well-being.

In the first few years, the *Sonja* delivered her catch to a nearby ship (the *Svaedfisken*) where whales were flensed and prepared for distribution. However, soon the whaling was conducted by the *Sonja* alone; after a whale was caught, it was towed to the nearest community, where flensing occurred on a suitable beach at low water. Flensers were allowed first choice of the meat and intestinal fat, followed by other community members; the blubber was shipped to Denmark where the oil was sold. Thus, community distribution of meat was free initially, but after a time the meat was sold in the communities at a nominal price.

The *Sonja* was replaced in 1950 with the larger *Sonja Kaligtoq*. This Danish whaling operation caught about thirty whales (though sometimes twice that number) in a season extending from May to late October. The catch was mostly fin whales and humpbacks, but occasionally sperm and blue whales were also taken. From 1954 onward, the whales were delivered to a single whaling station where the meat and mattak were frozen for distribution and sale throughout Greenland.

In addition to this Danish initiative, community-based whaling became revitalized in Greenland starting in 1948 when some fishing-boat owners installed harpoon cannons on their boats. Hunting occurred for minke, fin, and humpback whales more particularly, with meat and mattak sold in nearby communities. Although some hunters in West Greenland continue to be interested in taking humpback whales, in the late 1980s the IWC reduced the humpback quota in Greenland to zero, so this form of coastal whaling is restricted to minke and fin whales.

FIGURE 22. Harpoon cannon used on a Greenlandic fishing boat, 1994.

MINKE WHALE HUNTING

Greenland

Hunting for minke whale in West and East Greenland is based on quotas decided by the International Whaling Commission. Quotas for aboriginal whalers are arrived at by considering the socioeconomic, cultural, and nutritional needs together with the regional abundance of the whales. The Greenland Home Rule authorities allocate these quotas (which during the 1990s have ranged from 110 to 175 each year) and regulate the hunts, including the proportion of the catch allowed to be taken by the cooperative rifle-based hunts from small boats and by fishing boats. The edible products from all hunts are distributed by means of traditional exchange and cash sales in local communities, and also sent to processing plants that freeze and package the meat before distributing it to retail outlets throughout Greenland.

Both the small-boat and fishing-boat minke whale hunts in Greenland are opportunistic, undertaken when a whale is sighted or, in the case of the collective hunt, when a sufficient number of small-boat hunters are available. In some communities, where hunters do not own larger fishing boats, several 5-metre skiffs with a crew of two (as commonly used in beluga and narwhal hunts) are employed in a cooperative hunt for minke whales. Rifles and hand-thrown harpoons are used in the hunt, and the minke is towed to land where flensing and distribution of the meat occurs.

Whale product distribution differs significantly in the small-boat collective hunt and in the fishing-boat hunt. In the small-boat hunts, equal shares are distributed to all those participating in the hunt after the whale has been cut up. In contrast, in a fishing-boat hunt, the largest portion (usually around half of the total) is allocated to the vessel to cover the cost of the hunt; the remaining shares go to the vessel owner, to his immediate family, and to crew members (who are usually also family members), with some portion also being shared with those helping at the flensing site.

Despite the opportunity that exists to sell whale products for cash, the high value accorded the meat and mattak in the domestic economy ensures that only a small amount of the personal share that individuals receive typically is in fact sold. However, the boat share in the fishing-boat hunt is necessarily sold to contribute to the cost of operating this commercial fishing boat.

In East Greenland, hunters usually take minke whale in a collective hunt using skiffs powered by outboard motors. Minke whale are common in the area

FIGURE 23. Meat and mattak shares of whale received by hunters involved with taking and flensing a whale. Kangaatsiaq municipality, Greenland, October 1989.

around Ittoqqortoormiut from mid-June until early October. Minke whaling generally occurs in August and September, and around eight whales are taken each year.

NARWHAL HUNTING

Canada

As commercial whaling for bowhead came to an end, small trading stations were established in north Baffin Island to obtain furs, skins, oil, and ivory from the Inuit; however, it was the trade in narwhal ivory that yielded the traders their greatest profit. The Inuit involved in this trade came to depend on a wide variety of imported goods acquired from traders in return for skins and ivory. Winter rations were often provided to Inuit families to ensure that hunters would be available to hunt seals and narwhal in the spring, and this trading system was quickly incorporated into the life and economy of the northern Baffin Island Inuit. The hunting of narwhal for oil, skins, and most importantly tusks, however, provided the basis of this relationship.

Narwhal continue to be hunted today for their mattak, meat, and tusks. Younger animals and females do not normally possess tusks, and are taken primarily for their meat and mattak. Three types of hunting are conducted presently by Inuit in northern Baffin Island: floe-edge hunting from mid-June to mid-July, ice-crack hunting from late July to early August, and open-water hunting from early August to late September. Hunting narwhal from the floe edge and in ice cracks involves the use of rifles, small boats, and harpoons attached by lines to floats. During the open-water hunts, narwhal are pursued cooperatively by several hunters in outboard-powered boats with the goal of driving the whales into shallower waters, where they are then shot.

Traditionally, narwhal were hunted in much the same manner as described above using kayaks (until the mid-1950s). Another hunting technique used in the past involved a number of hunters shooting narwhal from steep rocks on the shore as they swam by, with several hunters in kayaks waiting nearby. Whenever a whale was shot from the rocks, the hunters would paddle out to harpoon the animal and tow it to shore.

Narwhal hunting in Canada's Arctic is confined almost exclusively to the east and north coasts of Baffin Island, with smaller numbers taken in northwest Hudson Bay, Foxe Basin, and Jones Sound. The combined annual quota, set by the Canadian authorities, for the communities of Pond Inlet and Arctic Bay (in northern Baffin Island) is 200 animals, while all other communities have a quota of less than fifty. Because of quota restrictions, there is a catch limit of five narwhal per year for each person. There are no restrictions on who may buy narwhal ivory, though tusks exported from Canada require an export permit to accord with Appendix II restrictions under CITES (Convention on International Trade in Endangered Species of Wild Fauna and Flora). Quota determinations reflect historic levels of take, local need, hunting pressures on this regional narwhal population that occurs elsewhere, and current size of the narwhal population.

Ever since the collapse of the seal-skin market, opportunities for Inuit hunters to earn an income have been limited. Trapping and hunting other furbearers, small-scale fisheries, and guiding sport hunters provide meaningful, though limited, incomes for hunters in some communities. In northern Baffin Island communities, some hunters may obtain a significant portion of their income in some years from the sale of narwhal tusks, which, on average, sell for about Can. $100 per foot (30 cm). Tusks longer than about 2.2 m sell for considerably more. Shorter and naturally damaged tusks are usually sold locally, to be made into ivory carvings.

The meat of narwhal has always been regarded principally as dog food, but it was also consumed raw, frozen, dried, or aged. As with the beluga, the oil of the narwhal is of superior quality compared to seal oil, and thus was used for heating and lighting purposes. The sinews of the narwhal were used in sewing waterproof boots and clothing. However, it was the mattak and the ivory tusk that were the most highly prized gifts of the narwhal. While the mattak was eaten fresh-raw or aged, the ivory tusks were fashioned into a variety of durable and functional tools including, most importantly, harpoon foreshafts, and the "eyes" (*oqsorq*) were used to attach individual dog traces to the sled.

Greenland

Narwhal ivory was bartered and exchanged among Inuit long before they had contact with Europeans. However, European merchants had been importing narwhal tusks into Europe since the Middle Ages, carefully concealing their origins to perpetuate the illusion that they were selling unicorn horn. The horn of this mythic creature not only conferred power and status to its possessor, but was believed to possess magical and medicinal qualities. It was the trade in narwhal ivory that apparently brought Inuit into close contact with the Norse in Greenland from the tenth through the thirteenth centuries, and later with Dutch and Danish whalers and traders during the seventeenth and eighteenth centuries, and with Danish traders well into the nineteenth century. As bow-heads declined in Baffin Bay, British whalers turned increasingly to hunting narwhal and bartering ivory with Greenlandic and Canadian Inuit.

Today, narwhal are hunted from kayaks in northern Greenland (Qaanaaq, Avanersuaq, and Upernavik districts) and from 5-metre skiffs or 10- to 12-metre cutters from Upernavik district south to Maniitsoq district. Netting in the fall or winter and ice-edge hunting is practiced from the northern hunting districts to Disko Bay. Narwhal are hunted from November through May from Aasiaat north to Disko Bay; only sporadically in winter in the Ilulissat district; during fall, winter, and spring in the Uummannaq district; and throughout the year in the northernmost districts. In many areas, local hunters' organizations have established by-laws regulating these hunts:

> In Avanersuaq we catch . . . narwhals from kayaks. We have very special rules about narwhal—one has to harpoon them before they can be shot when one goes on a narwhal hunt in the fiords near our area. . . . In the ice-free period the area is completely closed to motorized craft. One has to use a harpoon. After 15 September, the rules no longer apply because it begins to get too cold to catch narwhal with a kayak due to the layer of ice that forms on the water. . . . In summer we catch mostly narwhals.
>
> *Ussarqak Qujaukitsoq, Qaanaaq, July 1995*

In East Greenland, narwhal are generally hunted from kayaks or from skiffs, although they are sometimes shot from shore or taken in nets. The products from the narwhal are particularly important in this region, as the hunts frequently take place when other food species are less available. About eighty narwhal are taken each year in East Greenland.

Narwhal (and also beluga) are hunted in winter ice-entrapments (*sassat*) throughout their normal distribution range. Rifles used in the hunts are 30.06 or 7.62 mm, with a heavier 375 Magnum used for fast kills during floe-edge hunting.

HUNTING FOR OTHER SMALL WHALES

Canada

At various locations along the coast of Labrador, Inuit hunt bottlenose dolphin and harbour porpoise. These are the common small whales, as beluga are only rarely encountered, on migration past the more northerly communities.

FIGURE 24. Narwhal being flensed. Disko Bay, Greenland, 1995.

Hunting, principally for bottlenose dolphins, takes place in late summer or fall from motorized skiffs or trapboats.

Greenland

Other small-toothed whales are currently taken in small numbers in Greenland, including killer whale, pilot whale, northern bottlenose whale, harbour porpoise, and two species of dolphin. There is a general prohibition on shooting calves or females accompanied by calves for all these, and other, cetacean species in Greenland.

The numbers of each of these species taken most years is quite small, with the exception of harbour porpoise taken in East Greenland and in south and central-western Greenland, where the largest numbers are taken in the Maniitsoq and Nuuk districts.

SUGGESTED READINGS

Caulfield, R. A. 1997. *Greenlanders, Whales and Whaling: Sustainability and Self-Determination in the Arctic*. Hanover, NH, and London: University Press of New England.

Dahl, J. 1990. Beluga Hunting in Saqqaq. *North Atlantic Studies* 2(1–2):166–69.

Feldman, K. 1986. Subsistence Beluga Hunting in Alaska: A View From Eschscholtz Bay (1). In: S. J. Langdon (ed.), *Contemporary Alaskan Native Economies*, pp. 153–71. Lanham, Md.: University Press of America.

Freeman, M. M. R., E. E. Wein, and D. E. Keith. 1992. *Recovering Rights: Bowhead Whales and Inuvialuit Subsistence in the Western Canadian Arctic*. Studies in Whaling No. 2, Occasional Paper No. 31, Canadian Circumpolar Institute, Edmonton.

Huntington, H. P., and N. I. Mymrin (eds.). 1996. *Traditional Ecological Knowledge of Beluga Whales: An Indigenous Knowledge Pilot Project in the Chukchi and Northern Bering Sea*. Anchorage, Alaska: Inuit Circumpolar Conference.

Krupnik, I. I. 1987. Bowhead vs. Gray Whale in Chukotka Aboriginal Whaling. *Arctic* 40(1):16–32.

Krupnik, I. 1993. *Arctic Adaptations: Native Whalers and Reindeer Herders of Northern Eurasia*. Hanover, NH, and London: University Press of New England.

Lucier, C. V., and J. M. VanStone. 1995. *Traditional Beluga Drives of the Iñupiat of Kotzebue Sound, Alaska*. Fieldiana Publication 1468. Chicago: Field Museum of Natural History.

McCartney, A. P. 1996. *Hunting the Largest Mammals: Native Whaling in the Western Arctic and Subarctic*. Studies in Whaling No. 3, Occasional Paper No. 36, Canadian Circumpolar Institute, Edmonton.

McGhee, R. 1974. *Beluga Hunters: An Archaeological Reconstruction of the History and Culture of the Mackenzie Delta Kittegaryumiut*. Newfoundland Social and Economic Studies 13, St. John's, Newfoundland.

Mitchell, E., and R. R. Reeves. 1981. Catch History and Cumulative Catch Estimates of Initial Population size of Cetaceans in the Eastern Canadian Arctic. *Report of the International Whaling Commission* 31:645–82.

Morseth, C. M. 1997. Twentieth-century changes in beluga whale hunting and butchering among the Kanigmiut of Buckland, Alaska. *Arctic* 50(3):241–55.

Pokiak, B. 1989. Tuktoyaktuk memories. *Inuktitut Magazine* No. 70.

Spencer, R. F. 1959. *The North Alaska Eskimo: A Study in Ecology and Society*. Washington, D.C.: Bureau of American Ethnology 171.

Stevenson, M. G. 1997. *Inuit Whalers and Cultural Persistence*. Toronto: Oxford University Press.

Stevenson, M. G., A. Madsen, and E. Maloney (eds.). 1997. *The Anthropology of Community-based Whaling in Greenland*. Studies in Whaling No. 4, Occasional Paper No. 42. Canadian Circumpolar Institute, Edmonton.

Stoker, S. W., and I. I. Krupnik. 1993. Subsistence whaling. In: J. J. Burns, J. J. Montague, and C.J. Cowles (eds.), *The Bowhead Whale*, pp. 579–629. Lawrence, Kans.: The Society for Marine Mammalogy.

Zagoskin, L. A. 1967. Lieutenant Zagoskin's travels in Russian America, 1842–1844. The first ethnographic and geographic investigations on the Yukon and Kuskokwim valleys of Alaska. In: H. N. Michael (ed.), *Anthropology of the North: Translations from Russian Sources* 7, Arctic Institute of North America. Toronto: University of Toronto Press.

CHAPTER THREE

Human Rights and the International Whaling Commission

Each culture has a dignity and value which must be respected and preserved. Every people has the right and the duty to develop its culture. In their rich variety and diversity, and in the reciprocal influence they exert on one another, all cultures form part of the common heritage of humanity.

Article 1, Declaration of the Principles of International Cultural Co-operation, UNESCO

The International Whaling Commission (IWC) exercises management authority over certain species of interest to Inuit whalers—namely, bowhead, fin, gray, humpback, and minke whales. The section that follows will discuss the international convention that established the IWC, together with a number of subsequent international agreements that relate to the sustainable use and management of living resources. In addition, a number of international human rights agreements that nearly all United Nations governments are expected to honour and promote will be mentioned. This chapter questions whether actions of a majority of member governments of the IWC are consistent with those same governments' legal obligations under the international whaling convention itself, as well as under various international human-rights and environmental treaties that, in most cases, these governments have pledged to uphold.

THE INTERNATIONAL WHALING TREATY

In 1946, fifteen whaling nations signed the International Convention for the Regulation of Whaling (ICRW), which established the International Whaling Commission (IWC) as the management agency that was to regulate the hunting of those large whales of interest to the commercial whaling industry. However, because some of these species (for example, bowhead, fin, gray, and humpback) were also of interest to aboriginal whalers, the IWC has exempted aboriginal whaling from regulations designed for the commercial whaling industry. To qualify for this exemption, aboriginal whalers' use of whale products is restricted to local use only. In earlier years, restrictions were placed on the use of modern technology, in addition to a requirement that those whaling were to be "aboriginal" persons; however, both these restrictions have since been lifted.

At the present time, some ambiguity exists in regard to allowing the sale of edible whale products. In fact, as members of fully monetized societies, most aboriginal whalers need money to finance their whaling activities, and for some, the product of the hunt provides them with a commodity that has market value, either locally or, in some cases, nationally. However, the Convention allows any nation to regulate its own whaling more strictly than provided for in the Convention, and only one country—the United States—has decided to do that. Thus, Alaskan whalers are not allowed to sell or buy edible bowhead products, though the United States recognizes that buying and selling of edible whale products occurs in other aboriginal whaling societies, and is allowed for under U.S. law.

The Convention makes no mention of relatively small-sized toothed whales, the so-called small cetaceans (such as beluga, narwhal, and dolphins), and though the IWC Scientific Committee gathers statistical and scientific information on these species, the IWC assumes no internationally recognized authority over the management of these small whales. Today, disagreement exists over whether IWC possesses, or lacks, legal competence to manage small cetaceans. Thus, some member nations seek to extend IWC jurisdiction over these small-toothed whales, while other members insist that IWC has no legal right to do so.

During the 1980s, with the rise of the environmental movement, IWC membership increased to about forty nations. At the present time, the large majority of voting members (now numbering about thirty) neither whale nor use whale products. In fact, this majority strongly opposes the killing of whales. However, the purpose of the IWC, according to the Preamble to the

Convention, is *"to conserve whales in order to allow the orderly development of the whaling industry."* In pursuit of that objective, the IWC is required under its rules of procedure to base its advice on *"the best scientific advice"* (Article V, para. 2) and *"to take into account the needs and concerns of the users and consumers of whale products"* (Article V, para. 2[b]). Unfortunately for the few nations still choosing to hunt whales and eat whale products, the majority of IWC members choose to ignore these guiding principles of the Convention.

The antiwhaling members of the IWC justify their current disregard for the Convention by claiming they are not required to observe the 1946 treaty as a result of recent changes in "world opinion" that now, in their view, oppose the killing of whales. Legally, however, the Convention still remains in effect, even if its objectives are ignored by the majority of IWC members. Indeed, there is nothing in the 1946 Convention to suggest that whales are other than a renewable resource to be used prudently by whalers and consumers of whale products. The present antiwhaling bloc of IWC countries could legalize their present actions by seeking to renegotiate and ratify a new international treaty that better reflects their current political objectives. However, to date, no such legal changes have occurred.

OTHER RELEVANT INTERNATIONAL INITIATIVES

The United Nations Convention on the Law of the Sea (UNCLOS), to which more than 120 nations are signatories, came into force in 1994, and, even before that, the provisions of UNCLOS influenced the way many nations came to think about marine affairs. Thus, for example, the wording concerning marine mammals contained in UNCLOS was copied without change into those parts of the United Nations Conference on Environment and Development's (UNCED) Agenda 21 dealing with whale management, and similarly into Resolution 19.63 at the 1994 IUCN General Assembly, which was also concerned with whales. The pertinent wording in each case is Article 65 in UNCLOS, which in part states:

> States shall cooperate with a view to the conservation of marine mammals and in the case of cetaceans [whales] shall in particular work through the appropriate international organizations for their conservation, management and study.

In regard to the above-mentioned provisions, the term *"appropriate international organizations"* makes it clear that no single management regime is being specified. Second, *"international"* in this Article includes regional as well as global organizations, as evidenced throughout the Convention by the expression *"international organizations, whether global or regional."* Third, the use of the term *"management"* suggests this function should be considered when deciding just how *"appropriate"* an international organization is. It could be argued that by adopting an antiwhaling or antiuse position, and by ignoring competent scientific advice, the IWC has adopted a highly questionable management approach. Such an approach contradicts the provisions and intent of the ICRW, as well as UNCLOS and more recent international agreements (for example, World Conservation Strategy, World Commission on Environment and Development (WCED), UNCED/Agenda 21, and the Convention on Biological Diversity), all of which promote the sustainable use of renewable resources.

Under the terms of UNCLOS, any nation that is not a member of IWC has the right to whale both on the high seas and up to 200 miles from its own coastline, subject only to whatever international agreements to which it is a party, or in the case of its own coastal whaling, subject to its own national regulations.

There are also a number of UN human-rights agreements that are relevant to the present whaling debate—for example, the UN International Covenant on Economic, Social, and Cultural Rights, which includes the following statements of principle:

> All people may, for their own ends, freely dispose of their natural wealth and resources without prejudice to any obligations arising out of international economic cooperation, based upon the principle of mutual benefit, and international law. *In no case may a people be deprived of their means of subsistence.*

> All people have the right to self-determination. By virtue of that right they freely determine their political status *and freely pursue their economic, social, and cultural development.* [*emphases added*]

Article 12 makes reference to the *"right of everyone to the enjoyment of the highest attainable standard of physical and mental health."* The importance of a full range of subsistence activities certainly contributes importantly to maintenance of both physical and mental health. Denying people access to important subsistence resources and to the means for improving their livelihood and standard of living by restricting trade in surplus produce will certainly prevent them from achieving higher standards of health.

Article 15(1) of this UN Covenant recognizes every person's right *"to take part in cultural life,"* which means that states should not, through their actions, prevent a person's participation in cultural activities. This seems particularly pertinent to whaling, which, in the case of Inuit, can be shown to be an integral part of their hunting culture and food culture in all regions they occupy.

Also to be considered is the International Covenant on Civil and Political Rights. This Covenant affirms people's right to hold opinions without interference, as well as the right to freedom of expression. These rights are not without limitations (referred to as "special duties and responsibilities"); thus, individuals should respect the rights or reputations of others, and should uphold the protection of public health or the moral order. Thus, actions taken by animal protectionists and governments that seek to deny Inuit and other groups of people the full expression of their rights as members of a hunting culture, and as consumers of customary foods only obtained by the exercise of these hunting rights, appear to be in violation of these Covenant prescriptions. According to Article 27:

> In those States in which ethnic, religious, or linguistic minorities exist, persons belonging to such minorities shall not be denied the right, in community with the other members of their group, to enjoy their own culture.

Allowing a people *"to enjoy their own culture"* appears to require governments to afford protection against interference by others who oppose lawful aspects of the minority group's culture. It also means that governments should not take actions that increase the minority group's exposure to harmful threats to their culture, nor encourage other members of society to continue or escalate their harmful actions.

In December 1992, the UN General Assembly adopted the Declaration on the Rights of Persons Belonging to National or Ethnic, Religious, and Linguistic Minorities (Resolution 47/135), a Declaration inspired by Article 27 of the International Covenant on Civil and Political Rights. According to Elaine Ward (in a 1993 study published by the Danish Centre for Human Rights), the fact that the Declaration was adopted without a vote indicates that the provisions have become part of international customary law.

As mentioned earlier, the influence exerted by the UN Convention on the Law of the Sea has resulted in similar wording being used in the international agreement (Agenda 21) resulting from the UN Conference on Environment and Development (UNCED). Thus, in respect to marine mammals, the wording of UNCLOS Article 65 appears unchanged as Paragraph 17.50 of Agenda 21. The drafting of Agenda 21 appears designed to accommodate regional marine mammal/whale management bodies; in Paragraph 17.49 (c) it is stated:

> [States recognized] the work of other organizations, such as the Inter-American Tropical Tuna Commission and the Agreement on Small Cetaceans in the Baltic and North Seas under the Bonn Convention, in the conservation, management, and study of cetaceans and other marine mammals.

Other paragraphs of Agenda 21 have relevance to the management of whaling in the Arctic; for example:

> States should take measures to increase the availability of marine living resources as human food. . . . [Paragraph 17.60]

> States should, where and as appropriate, ensure adequate coordination and co-operation...between subregional, regional and global intergovernmental fisheries bodies. [Paragraph 17.63]

> Where such [sub-regional, regional and global fisheries bodies] do not exist, States should, as appropriate, cooperate to establish such organizations. [Paragraph 17.64]

> Coastal States, individually or through bilateral and/or multilateral cooperation . . . should . . . :

> b) implement strategies for the sustainable use of marine living resources, taking into account the special needs and interests of small-scale artisanal fisheries, local communities and indigenous people to meet human nutritional and other development needs . . .

> g) enhance the productivity and utilization of their marine living resources for food and income. [Paragraph 17.84]

> Coastal States should support the sustainability of small-scale artisanal fisheries. To this end, they should, as appropriate:

> b) recognize the rights of small-scale fishworkers and the special situation of indigenous people and local communities, including their right to utilization . . . on a sustainable basis. [Paragraph 17.86]

> Coastal States should ensure that in the . . . implementation of international agreements on the development or conservation of marine living resources, the interests of local communities and indigenous peoples are taken into account, in particular their right to subsistence. [Paragraph 17.87]

Elsewhere in Agenda 21, further explicit recognition is given both to the value of traditional fisheries and to the importance of incorporating traditional knowledge of marine living resources into national legislation and planning, as well as the need to consider indigenous rights to subsistence when negotiating future international agreements on marine resources.

Finally, with respect to indigenous communities' rights, Agenda 21 calls on states to establish a process to empower indigenous people through the recognition of traditional management practices, and protection *"from activities that are environmentally unsound or that indigenous people concerned consider to be socially and culturally inappropriate"* [Chapter 26, Subparagraph 26.3]. Agenda 21 also commits the United Nations to support indigenous people's traditional resource-management systems, and to encourage their sustainable use of biological resources [Chapter 16, Paragraph 16.7]. Thus Principle 22 of Agenda 21 states:

> Indigenous peoples and their communities and other local communities have a vital role in environmental management and development because of their knowledge and traditional practices. States should recognize and duly support their identity, culture, and interests and enable their effective participation in the achievement of sustainable development.

During UNCED, in Rio de Janeiro, the Convention on Biological Diversity (CBD) was open for signature; the CBD entered into force on December 29, 1993, and by late 1996, 161 nations had ratified the Convention. The philosophy of the CBD closely follows that of The World Conservation Strategy and the Brundtland Report, namely to promote:

- The conservation of biological diversity

- The sustainable use of living resources

- The fair and equitable sharing of the benefits arising from use of these resources

To achieve these results, the CBD urges a cooperative approach based on partnerships among different sectors of society with interests in these conservation and social goals. It links the achievement of such goals with the attainment of beneficial social and economic outcomes.

The preamble of the CBD recognizes the *"close and traditional dependence of many indigenous and local communities . . . on biological resources . . . ,"* with Article 8 (j) calling for *"respect, preservation, and maintenance of indigenous and local communities."*

Article 10 seeks to *"encourage customary use of biological resources in accordance with traditional cultural practices that are compatible with conservation or sustainable use requirements,"* while Article 11 states that governments *"shall, as far as possible and as appropriate, adopt economically and socially sound measures that act as incentives for the conservation and sustainable use of components of biological diversity."*

The 1991 World Conservation Strategy (entitled Caring for the Earth: A Strategy for Sustainable Living) was produced and promoted by the World Conservation Union (IUCN), the UN Environment Program (UNEP), and the World Wide Fund for Nature (WWF). Many national governments have based national conservation programmes on the principles espoused by the World Conservation Strategy. These principles include improving the quality of human life, enabling communities to care for their own environments, and conserving the Earth's vitality and diversity.

With respect to improving the quality of human life, the Strategy stresses the importance of enabling people to realize their potential and lead lives of dignity and fulfillment, and of people's having access to resources needed for a decent standard of living. It states that local communities must have a part in the management of local wild resources and should benefit from the economic returns such resources afford.

With respect to marine resources in particular, the Strategy states that in allocating the rights to use such resources, particular emphasis should be given to the interests of local communities. In calling for strengthening international cooperation in such matters, it especially stresses the importance of regional cooperation.

The International Labour Organization (ILO) has developed its Convention on Indigenous and Tribal Peoples, No. 169 (1989), which came into force in 1991. Although at the present time Convention 169 has been ratified by few states, central parts of it, in respect to self-development and cultural integrity (which are both relevant to the whaling issue), achieved a global consensus at the UNCED Rio Summit in 1992.

Convention 169 recognizes indigenous peoples' rights, among others, to self-development, cultural and institutional integrity, and environmental security. In the Convention, reference is made to indigenous peoples' ownership and possession of the total environment and protection from unwanted intrusion from outsiders.

The main theme of the Convention includes recognition of indigenous peoples' right to continue to own and manage every part of the ecosystem (excepting minerals) that they have traditionally used. Indeed, in respect to renewable resources, the Convention affirms that they belong fully under indigenous control.

The Convention enjoins states not to undertake actions *"contrary to the freely expressed wishes of the peoples concerned,"* with any state actions preceded *"by good faith [consultations] with the objective of achieving [their] agreement or consent."*

RECENT ACTIONS AT THE INTERNATIONAL WHALING COMMISSION

In view of these varied international agreements and principles intended to guide states' actions toward diverse peoples, how are whaling people's interests, in fact, being treated within the context of IWC decisions? Generally speaking, in more recent years, Inuit whalers in Alaska, Chukotka, and Greenland have been treated well in comparison with other whalers (Canadian Inuit are not subject to IWC jurisdiction, Canada having left the IWC in 1982).

Although by some measures (for instance, increases in quotas for bowhead whales in Chukotka and minke whales in West Greenland in 1997) there appears to be greater accommodation of the needs of Inuit whaling communities, the future nevertheless remains uncertain. The reason for such uncertainty is that political changes occurring in any member country can alter that nation's position toward whaling quite suddenly and drastically. For example, at the 1996 IWC meeting, two aboriginal whaling groups made requests for modest quotas for cultural, social, economic, and nutritional purposes.

In the first case, aboriginal whalers in the Chukotka region of Siberia unsuccessfully requested five bowhead whales. One country that opposed the Chukotkan request was Australia, which appears to have reversed the position it formally announced at the 1994 IWC meeting in these words:

The strong commitment we have to recognition of the continuation of access of traditional communities to whaling and whale products really arises from our dedication to concern for traditional peoples. . . . We are aware of how strong and, at the same time, how fragile can be the forces that maintain community structure and cohesion, and how important those issues are, particularly to traditional people in coastal environments. We continue to examine these issues closely, and examine each of these cases in that context.

There are probably no traditional peoples today who illustrate more starkly the concerns expressed by the Australian commissioner. The Chukotkan whalers, facing the near-total collapse of the regional economy, are experiencing very extreme—indeed, life-threatening—conditions, which were ably communicated to the 1996 IWC meeting by the Russian government delegation. To illustrate the serious nature of the situation, the following message (dated April 2, 1996) was passed from Deputy V. I. Gayulskii (of the Parliament of the Russian Federation) to the Vice-Premier of the Russian Federation:

> There is a disastrous situation connected with the provision of food to the indigenous population of Chukotka. There is a vicious circle whereby the indigenous population has no means of existence and no economic support. On a number of farms people do not get their wages for more than a year due to decreased production and problems associated with marketing products like meat, fur, marine mammal fats etc., and the prices for imported foods in rural stores constantly increase, making these foods virtually inaccessible. This causes suffering, particularly of children, which threatens irreversible consequences regarding the survival . . . of the indigenous people.
>
> In this critical situation the indigenous minorities have only one way of survival—to get back to the traditional subsistence foods, to use the biological resources of the territory. The problem is the restoration of the quota for the bowhead whale, the traditional food item of coastal Chukchi and Eskimos. . . . Studies of the last years, particularly those involving the indigenous population of Chukotka, have demonstrated that the stock has been restored and is now quite favourable. . . .
>
> *Letter signed by V. M. Etylin, Vice President, Association of Indigenous Peoples of the North, Siberia, and Far East of the Russian Federation*

The significance of this request is that it is a plea for five bowhead whales in a region where the indigenous people were provided a quota of 140 gray whales (but which, for technical reasons, they were not able to take at that time). However, it is the bowhead whale alone that provides the basis for traditional practices, and it is these cultural traditions that these marine hunters were seeking to revive, to provide guidance and strength in their search for social improvement. Thus, in a February 1995 letter to marine-mammal hunters in Chukotka, we read:

> We want to unite our efforts during this critical economic period . . . to revive our ancient language, culture, and tradition as marine mammal hunters and collect and pass on our skills as traditional resource users. . . . No one will

solve these problems for us. We must think about the protection of our ancient culture as marine mammal hunters. This is the basic lifestyle of the people of the Bering Straits of Chukotka. Only in this way can we save ourselves as an independent people and pass on to our descendants our traditional way of life.

> *Signed by an initiating group of nine individuals, including*
> *the Chairman of the Society of Chukotkan Eskimos*

However, at the 1997 IWC meeting, Australia and other nations opposing the 1996 request for five bowhead whales appeared to have reconsidered their position. In 1997, in exchange for reducing their annual gray-whale quota by twenty whales, the Chukotkans obtained five bowhead whales each year from a combined Chukotkan–Alaskan quota of 280 bowheads over the period 1998–2002. However, to maintain its uncompromising opposition to any expansion of whaling, Australia, at the 1997 IWC meeting, explicitly dissociated itself from the consensus agreement to allow the Chukotkan gray-whale quota to be shared with the Makah Indian nation in the United States.

The 1996 IWC meeting also considered three other aboriginal subsistence whaling issues. One was a minor matter of no consequence in itself, but was significant in relation to yet another Commission outcome in 1996. The minor matter was an "infraction" reported by the U.S. government, when Alaskan whalers killed two gray whales in the absence of a U.S. allocation for this species.

The United States formerly had a quota of ten gray whales, but it voluntarily surrendered that quota a few years ago. For that reason, it reported the capture of two gray whales as an infraction. However, the IWC Infractions Committee did not see this hunt as constituting an infraction, observing that the IWC does not award quotas to individual countries, but rather sets quotas on what are considered to be management "stocks" of any particular species. Thus, in this Alaskan case, there was no infraction because the IWC had allocated a quota of 140 gray whales to be taken each year, and at that time the Chukotkan whalers only took 80 to 85 gray whales from the quota, thus leaving 55 to 60 to be taken by others.

This nonissue is mentioned because it illustrates the inconsistency and disregard for its own rules that characterizes IWC performance, and hence the uncertainty that Inuit whalers are required to cope with at each IWC annual meeting. This inconsistency was highlighted during the same IWC meeting, when another U.S. whaling people, the Makah Nation of Washington State, requested a quota of five gray whales from the same stock as that hunted by Alaskan and Chukotkan whalers.

In times past, the Makah were among the most accomplished whalers in the Pacific Northwest. Reclaiming their whaling traditions has required a wait of many years, but community leaders now believe the time has arrived to restore that cherished part of their cultural heritage. The Makah are the only Indian tribe in the United States with a formal treaty that guarantees them the right to hunt whales. Recognition of that treaty responsibility, together with the democratic process by which the Makah tribal government determined Makah support for the proposal to resume whaling, gave the U.S. government no legitimate grounds to withhold its support from the Makah request for a quota of five nonendangered (and now fully recovered) California gray whales.

In support of their request to the IWC for a small quota, the Makah produced a comprehensive report that explained their cultural need to resume whaling at this time. However, once again, a small number of countries (including those opposing the Chukotkan request for five bowhead whales) blocked the Makah request for five gray whales. The U.S. request to succeed required a three-quarter majority, so, faced with opposition from several antiwhaling IWC delegations, the United States withdrew the request, rather than have it defeated by the IWC antiwhaling bloc. It may be asked: why did the United States even seek a vote on this particular hunt, when earlier in the same meeting it was told (by the Infractions Committee) that the existing gray-whale quota more than accommodated U.S. whaling needs?

The inconsistency in the two U.S. actions taken in regard to gray whales reflects the capricious, and hence unpredictable, nature of IWC actions—actions that result from political considerations taking place both inside and outside of the IWC itself. Whalers, being in a distinct minority, commonly find themselves subject to political actions that, irrespective of the merits of their requests, prove difficult or impossible to treat reasonably—as the Makah found to their dismay, cost, and better understanding of the IWC process.

A third matter affected aboriginal whalers at the 1996 IWC, though it was a matter that arguably fell outside of IWC jurisdiction, as it involved a non-member of the IWC. Nevertheless, it became an issue because of the needs of one nation's purely domestic political agenda. To satisfy these domestic needs, the U.S. delegation tabled a resolution directed against Canada for issuing a licence permitting the Inuit to hunt a single bowhead whale in 1996 in the eastern Canadian Arctic. Canada, as a nonmember of the IWC, has no reason to seek IWC permission for taking a management decision adequately treated under Canadian law and whaling policy. Even *members* of IWC are allowed to act independently of any IWC decisions (by lodging a reservation against majority decisions that are not in their own national interest); presumably non-members are even less bound by IWC decisions.

The questionable propriety, if not legality, of these actions at this one IWC meeting, which was by no means an exceptional meeting, does bring into question the reasonableness of the organization's current actions. Indeed, the record of the past several years makes questionable the ability of the International Whaling Commission to act with fairness, honesty, and integrity, when the interests of whalers is being decided by those rigidly opposed to the catching and eating of whales. The whaling convention [ICRW] is the international agreement that sets the objectives, together with the means to achieve these objectives, for the IWC to follow. Article V(2) of the ICRW provides explicit guidance on the means to be taken to *"provide for the conservation, development and optimum utilization of whale resources"* while taking *"into consideration the interests of the consumers of whale products and the whaling industry."*

The legality of several actions taken by the IWC has recently been questioned. In regard to one such action taken to prevent a resumption of whaling (by declaring a large area of the southern oceans to be a whale sanctuary), a distinguished legal scholar has concluded:

> Article V [of the ICRW] requires that changes necessary for carrying out the objectives and purposes of the ICRW be based upon scientific findings. It is concluded that the sanctuary is not necessary for carrying out the objectives and purposes of the ICRW . . . [and] that the decision was not based on scientific findings. . . . The proposal for the sanctuary and the decision to establish it were not consistent with the Commission's own guidelines. The conclusion is that the Commission's decision is unlawful under the ICRW and ultra vires.
>
> *William T. Burke, in* Ocean Development and International Law 27, *p. 315, 1996*

This legal expert further notes, in regard to IWC actions in overriding the requirements of the ICRW when these requirements obstruct the majority's antiwhaling agenda:

> Reinterpretation of an agreement which defeats the major purpose of the parties, and substitutes a purpose not shared by all parties and actively rejected by some, is not a permissible means of interpretation under contemporary international law.
>
> *Burke 1996, p. 323*

A Greenlander, familiar with the politics and caprice of the IWC, has, in relation to such irregularities, observed:

> How well we recognize this from the IWC, where the Greenlanders get their minke whale quotas, but the Norwegian [do] not. After a good many years of working with the IWC, let me now publicly admit that I have never yet been able to see any other significant difference between minke whale hunts of Greenland and the Norwegian small scale coastal whaling, than that of the race of the harpooners.
>
> *Finn Lynge, Copenhagen, January 1996*

Actions at the IWC appear to violate at will the legal requirements of its own Convention, without providing any recourse to the aggrieved party or parties. Furthermore, through prohibiting trade conducted outside of local communities, and by failing to recognize and protect the integral role that trade plays in sustaining coastal people's social and cultural relations and development, the actions of the IWC violate rights that the UN Covenant on Social, Economic, and Cultural Rights seeks to protect. Further, the IWC is not legally competent to take such actions, as the Norwegian IWC Commissioner was required to remind IWC Commissioners during the 1996 meeting:

> . . . it is very serious that attempts are consistently being made to extend IWC's competence and thereby our treaty obligations beyond the provisions of the Convention. The IWC is not the competent body for trade issues. WTO [the World Trade Organization] and CITES [the Convention on International Trade in Endangered Species] are the international organizations recognized in the trade area. . . . It is also serious for this organization that the majority is trying to introduce responsibilities on all members of a treaty. . . . It is a well established practice in the U.N. that a majority cannot force a country to comply with a resolution which that country has voted against.

Recent UN agreements seeking to protect biological diversity and environmental values also stress the role that resource users should play in realizing these conservation goals. Actions at the IWC appear designed to antagonize resource users by trivializing their community needs, their culture, and their socioeconomic and health problems, problems that in many cases would, at the very least, be partially ameliorated by allowing small sustainable takes of locally available whales. Again, recognition of the rights of the users to benefit from sustainable resource use, which is held to be an integral part of the solution to environmental problems, is ignored by IWC in the pursuit of more narrowly defined political goals that are unrelated both to whale management, and, less narrowly, to broader conservation objectives.

It appears evident that, in the view of the majority at IWC meetings, some people's human rights, together with broadly based conservation goals, to say nothing of respect for international law, have far less importance than the rights of whales to enjoy protection from being hunted.

SUGGESTED READINGS

Burke, W. T. 1994. *The New International Law of Fisheries: UNCLOS 1982 and Beyond* (Marine mammals, pp. 255–302). Oxford: Clarendon Press.

———. 1996. Editorial Comment. *Ocean Development and International Law* 27:315–26.

Caring for the Earth: A Strategy for Sustainable Living. 1991. Gland, Switzerland: IUCN/UNEP/WWF.

IUCN Inter-Commission Task Force on Indigenous Peoples. 1997. *Indigenous Peoples and Sustainability: Cases and Actions.* Utrecht: International Books.

Nordic Council of Ministers. 1996. *Indigenous Peoples Production and Trade—Seminar in Copenhagen,* 15–17 January 1996. TemaNord 1996:553, Copenhagen.

Ward, E. 1993. *Indigenous Peoples Between Human Rights and Environmental Protection—Based on an Empirical Study of Greenland.* Copenhagen: The Danish Centre for Human Rights.

World Commission on Environment and Development. 1987. *Our Common Future [The Report of the World Commission on Environment and Development, the Brundtland Report].* Oxford: Oxford University Press.

The World Conservation Strategy. 1980. Gland, Switzerland: IUCN/UNEP/WWF.

CHAPTER FOUR

A Review of Whaling Management Regimes

ALASKA

Whaling in Alaska is a federal responsibility, with the federal authorities committed to creating comanagement structures in order to bring whalers' knowledge and concerns into the decision-making process. The principal national legislation controlling whaling in the United States is the Marine Mammal Protection Act (MMPA), which, in effect, bans the killing of whales. However, the MMPA exempts indigenous Alaskan whalers from this ban, provided the taking is not wasteful and is for subsistence purposes. The MMPA also allows the sale of whale products that are surplus to immediate needs. The United States, however, accepts the overriding authority of the IWC with respect to the hunting of bowhead and gray whales by U.S. citizens, so that comanagement of bowhead whales is, for example, subject to IWC restrictions both on the number of whales allowed to be taken and on the distribution and sale of edible whale products by Alaskan hunters.

The Alaska Eskimo Whaling Commission

A management history of Alaskan bowhead whaling includes generations of sustainable indigenous hunting, a disruptive era of uncontrolled outside exploitation in the nineteenth and early twentieth centuries, conflicts over whaling in the 1970s and 1980s, and growing recognition of sustainable whaling through cooperative management in the 1990s. Today, Inuit people in

FIGURE 25. The "blanket toss" during Nalukataq festivities. Barrow, Alaska, June 1988.

Alaska have a management regime that most hunters view as responsive to their needs and that many outsiders regard as a model for effective management. Bowhead whaling today is managed through a cooperative agreement between the U.S. government and the Alaska Eskimo Whaling Commission (AEWC). The AEWC is made up of whaling captains who represent their communities in decisions made about quota allocations, appropriate rules for whaling, and the development and use of new technologies.

> In terms of management, we feel that we adapt to the changes and trends. . . . But in terms of management, I think it is fair that every three years, along with the nine other whaling communities, Barrow gets together in a convention to distribute and allocate the bowhead whales according to what the IWC has provided. In terms of management, it's fair, it's concrete, and it's accepted in the ten whaling communities in Alaska. Let the local entities regulate themselves in that respect.
>
> *Delbert Rexford, Barrow, April 1995*

The IWC allocates bowhead quotas to Alaskan Inuit under its "aboriginal subsistence whaling" provision. This enables indigenous peoples to hunt certain species of whale under IWC quotas to satisfy cultural and nutritional needs. The IWC's Scientific Committee now accepts that the Bering–Chukchi–Beaufort Sea bowhead stock numbers in excess of 8,000 animals, and is increasing, after current hunting is factored into the calculation, at a rate of about 3 percent annually. The quota for the bowhead hunt was 204 whales landed in the four-year period from 1995 to 1998, and 280 for the next five-year period (with five whales per year allocated to the Chukotkan whalers).

It is recognized, however, that not every attempt to land a whale will be successful, so each year Alaskan whalers are allowed a larger number of "strikes" than the number of whales they require to land. A "strike" occurs when an explosive grenade or some other potentially lethal projectile is fired into a whale. Hunting in the year must cease when the allotted number of strikes or landed whales has been reached, whichever number is reached first. In recent years, the total number of strikes allowed was 68 in 1995, 67 in 1996, 66 in 1997, and 65 in 1998. Up to ten unused strikes can be added to the quota in a subsequent year. At the present time, between 65 and 75 percent of struck whales are successfully landed, a success rate that has shown steady improvement in recent years.

The annual quota allocation of strikes (for the years 1995 through 1997) for each of the whaling villages was as follows (the number of whaling crews in 1994 is indicated in parentheses):

Savoonga	(23)	6
Gambell	(24)	8
Little Diomede	(4)	2
Wales	(5)	2
Kivalina	(9)	4
Point Hope	(20)	10
Wainwright	(13)	7
Barrow	(44)	22
Nuiqsut	(10)	4
Kaktovik	(9)	3

Alaskan Inuit practiced sustainable whaling for generations before the arrival of Euro-Americans. The strong spiritual basis of the hunt, a relatively small indigenous population, limited technology, and other factors kept the take of bowheads well within sustainable limits. However, overexploitation of the bowhead by Yankee and other whalers in the latter part of the nineteenth century severely depleted bowhead numbers. Despite this, indigenous bowhead whaling continued into the twentieth century. Inuit people were allowed to take bowheads without limits, even after enactment of the MMPA of 1972 and the U.S. Endangered Species Act of 1973. Under the latter, bowheads were listed as endangered because of the severe depletion caused by nineteenth century commercial whaling.

In the early 1970s, a significant increase was seen in Inuit hunting efforts. Between 1970 and 1977, the number of whaling crews increased from 44 to 100 (today it is around 160), and the average number of whales landed annually during this period doubled, from about 15 per year to about 30 per year. At the same time, however, the number of bowheads struck but not actually landed and utilized increased significantly—caused, some suggested, by inexperienced captains and crews as well as by increased competition among crews.

The increased catch of bowheads attracted the attention of outsiders for the first time in the early 1970s. This was a time of growing attention to environmental concerns in many Western countries, and with whales having been adopted as a symbol of resource overexploitation, all whaling activities worldwide were now subject to growing scrutiny.

In 1977, the International Whaling Commission called for a total ban on bowhead whaling. The U.S. government, at the time leading the global antiwhaling offensive at the IWC, did not object. Alaskan Inuit hunters were totally unprepared for this news, and were shocked and offended:

> If you imagine what happened, what reaction came about in 1977 when [hunters] were asked to stop whaling—it was incomprehensible. And people were deeply hurt. Men and women were all crying. And it still affects me very deeply that we were hurt by something like that.
>
> *Marie Adams Carroll, Barrow*

Chairman Burton Rexford of the AEWC later recounted his reactions to the ban:

> The censuring of the whale hunt was forced on us, it was and is the most incomprehensible difficulty we have yet endured. We, the Iñupiat people, by our own hands did not cause the whale population to become depleted. The Westerners told us that the whales' population was decreasing. We have not seen their numbers decrease. However, if their numbers are smaller, it is because of the Westerners' influence here in the Arctic. The Iñupiat people have unjustly been blamed for killing off the whale as a species.

At issue were bowhead biologists' population estimates that suggested that there were only from 600 to 2,000 animals at that time (1977). Inuit elders argued that the scientists had seriously underestimated the number of whales in the population because they counted only whales observed in open water near shore-fast ice, and they failed to count the whales migrating hundreds of kilometres further offshore. Hunters estimated that the number of whales ranged around 7,000, and also pointed to a variety of gaps in scientific knowledge, including that having to do with migration behaviour and fertility, which cast doubt on the wisdom or necessity of the ban. In a court brief filed to object to the government's actions, hunters argued that:

> . . . the simplistic management approach of the IWC is not satisfactory to the Inuit, nor should it be to the general public. A truly scientific attitude about the bowhead whale should be to examine the specie [sic] condition explicitly and in depth. When the facts are available, a national specie management policy can be developed. Without such facts, any government policy of "whale management" is likely to be wrong and counter-productive.

Inuit hunters reacted by forming the Alaska Eskimo Whaling Commission (AEWC) in August 1977, thereby uniting the nine whaling communities (Little Diomede joined AEWC in 1992). The AEWC was designed to:

- Preserve and enhance the marine resource of the bowhead whale, including the protection of its habitat

- Protect Eskimo subsistence bowhead whaling

- Protect and enhance the Eskimo culture, traditions, and activities associated with bowhead whales and bowhead whaling

- Undertake research and educational activities related to bowhead whales

The AEWC's membership consists of voting and nonvoting members; the former are registered whaling captains from each whaling community, while nonvoting members are whaling crew members. Each community elects one representative to serve on the Board of Commissioners, which meets annually. The Board elects a chairman and other officers, and hires a small staff.

After threatening to disregard the IWC imposition of a zero quota, Inuit hunters were able to reach an interim agreement with the U.S. government in December 1977. Thus, in 1978, the IWC agreed to a modified quota of eighteen whales struck or twelve landed, whichever was reached first. It appeared as though Inuit cultural and nutritional needs associated with whaling were recognized.

This interim agreement was replaced in 1981 by a comprehensive cooperative agreement (later amended) with the U.S. government's National Oceanic and Atmospheric Administration (NOAA). Under this agreement, NOAA delegates authority to the AEWC for allocating quotas and managing the hunt without the presence of federal agents in whaling communities. The AEWC agreed to manage the hunt consistent with a management plan that specifies the arrangements for the hunt and penalties for any violations. The agreement also calls for a comprehensive scientific research programme on the bowhead.

A more recent amendment to the cooperative agreement states that the AEWC Management Plan *"will provide that the meat and products of whales taken in the subsistence hunt must be used exclusively for native consumption and may not be sold or offered for sale."* At the same time, the AEWC has sought financial compensation for whaling captains, through income tax relief, to offset certain expenses incurred by engaging in the bowhead hunt.

The goal of the bowhead research programme, according to the North Slope Borough's Chief Scientist, Tom Albert, was to make the case for continued whaling based on the best science available:

Our research has to be very good, because on the one hand we have the [oil] industry people who we've been beating up on who would really like to find something wrong with it, and the IWC people, some of whom would like to find something wrong. I spend a lot of my time trying to make sure that projects are well designed and stand up to appropriate review.

Barrow, April 1995

Moreover, the AEWC's research program is designed to incorporate the knowledge of experienced whaling captains. According to Tom Albert:

We try to combine local knowledge with scientific knowledge. Probably the best example of this [was] in 1981, when we actually took over the counting process. We then basically designed the whole research programme around what a few very senior Eskimo hunters told us, and in particular one man, Harry Brower, Sr. He very carefully took me under his wing and explained about how the animals move through the ice. [That] didn't make a whole lot of sense to an ordinary biologist, because our viewpoint is "I'm afraid of ice; I'm sure these whales are afraid of ice." But in reality, these whales are not afraid of ice, and that's the key thing. He knew it and the rest of us didn't. We have spent about fourteen years of research and many, many millions of dollars to determine whether or not he was accurate, and he was right every time.

Barrow, April 1995

Today, the North Slope Borough manages a budget of more than $2 million annually for research and management related to bowhead whaling. About $500,000 of that annually goes to the operation of the AEWC. Under the terms of the cooperative agreement, research continues on the bowhead population census and on certain other topics. The AEWC continues its Weapons Improvement Program, to increase the efficiency and safety of existing weapons used in the bowhead hunt.

The Alaska Beluga Whale Committee

For generations, Inuit hunters have relied on the careful observations of experienced hunters, culturally based rules and prohibitions, and spiritual guidance in ensuring that beluga and other living resources were used sustainably. However, the MMPA, enacted by the U.S. Congress in 1972, now serves as the basis for management discussions and attempts at cooperation between Inuit and other indigenous Alaskan hunters, as well as federal and state resource managers. The MMPA placed a moratorium on the take of marine mammals in U.S. waters, though an exemption for Alaska Natives allows takes for subsistence

Current Bowhead Management Concerns in Alaska

As far as the IWC goes, there are countries that don't want us to go whaling. When it comes to management, they review [our scientific data] every year [but] it always manages to pass. I think we have contributed a lot to the world, as far as the resources and species go. I think that's a very good model to follow. I would highly recommend [that others] tap into the traditional knowledge and management.

Burton Rexford, Barrow, April 1995

The crisis in bowhead whaling management of the late 1970s and 1980s has now given way to elaboration and refinement of the cooperative management regime developed both by the AEWC and by federal and state agencies. While the immediate conflict over the sustainability of the hunt has eased following scientific evidence that the bowhead population continues to steadily increase in size, some serious conflicts remain and potential new issues also threaten. Within the IWC context, there are still some who oppose all forms of whaling, believing that whales are "uniquely special" within the animal kingdom and, therefore, that individual animals should be protected from being killed.

However, today there is arguably greater acceptance in the IWC that justifiable cultural and nutritional needs are met by continued aboriginal whaling, though some countries stubbornly persist in believing (and acting as though) whaling is unnecessary, indeed unjustified, in the modern world. In this mixture of views, a majority appears to accept the need for bowhead whaling—provided that it is nonwasteful and occurs at levels the scientists agree is sustainable. There is concern among whalers that creating a whale sanctuary in the southern hemisphere (without any scientific justification for doing so) could lead to similar efforts to close out whaling in the Arctic. When the IWC adopted the Antarctic sanctuary in 1994, some antiwhaling groups immediately afterward made a statement that "The Arctic is next!"

More troubling to the whalers, because it was backed by a majority of member nations, was a resolution passed at the IWC in 1994 that proposed that initial steps be taken to start considering a new aboriginal-subsistence whaling management scheme. This new scheme would set catch quotas and enforce regulations on Inuit whaling. The IWC is currently developing a Revised Management Scheme (RMS) intended to very stringently control commercial whaling. Included in the RMS is a "catch limit algorithm," a mathematical procedure for calculating very conservative catch quotas, having the probable effect of closing down a number of small-scale commercial operations. The 1994 resolution recommends that a similar approach be applied to IWC aboriginal whaling. Certainly, application of this very conservative management scheme to bowhead whaling in Alaska would result in a zero quota. At this time, the AEWC is actively working with scientists to develop an alternative management procedure that will allow them to continue hunting at the required levels.

We knew that as soon as [the IWC] got done with other species they would turn their attention to us, which they're now doing. They want to develop a revised Aboriginal Whaling Scheme. We know that some people are going to propose that the . . . commercial whaling [scheme] be turned to apply to the aboriginal species. [But] . . . we are going to the IWC with the idea of resisting any effort to apply a very gross technique . . . to handling bowhead data. We want a technique that uses all the bowhead whale data and treats it properly, [and] the method we now have . . . takes account of all bowhead data, puts it in, and spits out a number that's reasonable.

Tom Albert, Barrow, April 1995

A second issue being pursued at the IWC is the difficult political issue of "humane killing" of whales. While there is no agreement on what constitutes "humane killing," there is agreement that new weapons can help to reduce the time-to-death in whaling. Thus, the AEWC has a Weapons Improvement Program that is adapting the penthrite grenade for use in the darting gun, with the first field trials using the new technology carried out in 1988 on eight bowheads. Penthrite grenades continue to be tested, with the view to their eventually being used exclusively for first strikes. According to the AEWC Chairman's 1995 Report, *"the AEWC has continued to work closely with [Norwegian weapons expert] Dr. Egil Øen in furthering the development of our penthrite projectile. The penthrite grenade continues to be a key component of our humane killing program."* The AEWC is also conducting training workshops aimed at improving the efficiency and safety of killing bowhead.

One other issue of importance is the value whaling captains place on local management and control. While Alaskan bowhead whaling clearly takes place under IWC quotas and through the cooperative agreement with the U.S. federal government, whaling captains believe that only they and the AEWC should speak on behalf of bowhead whaling in national and international settings, and not those who lack whaling experience—even if they are indigenous people themselves. Barrow whaling captain Arnold Brower, Jr. in 1995 insisted, *"It is critical that whaling captains and presidents [of local whaling associations] are the delegates at these meetings. Let's make sure that the person is a very knowledgeable person: a whaling captain and a local chairman of a community whaling association."*

The bowhead whalers believe they have devised an excellent management regime, one that is working well, and with every promise of improvement in the future:

I think the management plan that the Alaska Eskimo Whaling Commission devised and the management agreement is certainly adequate. We've negotiated a management plan that pretty much leaves a lot of the management of how the hunt takes place to the AEWC. And managing the hunt ourselves has provided a lot of incentives to do better in the management of the hunt.

Jacob Adams, Barrow, April 1995

A final issue raised by several Alaskan Inuit has to do with the need for passing on the knowledge and traditions of elders and whaling captains to young people. In responding to a question about factors that could undermine whaling in the future, Marie Adams Carroll responded that:

Like anything else, I guess we all have to take responsibility and as Inuit I think we have to take that responsibility to maintain the culture. Unless we do that, then there wouldn't be anything to maintain. I think the thing we need to pay attention to is our children, whether we are passing on all that we have learned from our elders, the knowledge and practices needed when we deal with the ice and the environment. Unless we teach those to our young people, I think that the biggest threat could come from us. Whether we like it or not, there is going to be outside pressures [but] I think as long as we maintain the spirit of our culture, we can manage.

Barrow, April 1995

and handicraft purposes. It placed federal management authority for beluga and other whale species in the hands of the National Marine Fisheries Service (NMFS).

In 1988, indigenous hunters in Alaska and Canada formed the Alaska and Inuvialuit Beluga Whale Committee (AIBWC) in response to growing awareness of shared concerns and increasing attention given to small cetaceans at the international level. Subsequently, in 1994 the AIBWC was restructured, and named the Alaska Beluga Whale Committee (ABWC). The ABWC continues to focus on conservation and management of beluga whales and their habitat, together with preservation of beluga-whale hunting in the Alaskan part of the animals' range. The committee's voting membership includes three representatives each from Alaska's North Slope, NANA (NANA Regional Corporation), Norton Sound, Yukon Delta, Kuskokwim, Bristol Bay, and Cook Inlet regions; the three regional representatives are to include two hunters and an at-large regional representative. In addition, voting members include two representatives each from the U.S. National Marine Fisheries Service, the Alaska Department of Fish and Game, the North Slope Borough, and others formally approved by the committee as a whole.

In December 1995, the ABWC adopted an Alaska Beluga Whale Management Plan that includes elements focusing on conservation, hunting and use of beluga by Alaska Natives, catch reporting and monitoring, public involvement in decision-making, research, and enforcement. The plan's overall goals are to maintain healthy populations of beluga whales in Alaskan waters, and to provide adequate subsistence take of beluga whales and protect hunting privileges for Alaskan subsistence hunters.

In addition to adopting the management plan, the ABWC has developed a statewide beluga-catch information system, supported by local beluga management committees in Norton Sound, Bristol Bay, and Cook Inlet. It has established beluga research priorities, including aerial surveys in Norton Sound, Bristol Bay, and the Chukchi Sea (1992–1996), genetic analysis to determine population discreteness, and contaminant studies.

The ABWC's significant efforts paralleled two important changes in 1994 to the MMPA having direct bearing on use of marine mammals by Alaskan aboriginal hunters. The first major change (Section 117) required the Secretary of Commerce to assess the health of every marine-mammal species and to develop "stock" assessments, including a determination whether or not the "stock" is considered "strategic." A "stock" is considered "strategic" if the "stock's" human-caused mortality is greater than an allowable "Potential Biological Removal" (PBR) level, if the "stock" is declining in a way that will likely lead to its listing as threatened under the Endangered Species Act (ESA), or if it is already listed as threatened, endangered, or depleted under the ESA. The PBR is defined as the maximum number of animals that may be removed from a marine mammal "stock" while allowing that "stock" to reach, or maintain, its optimum sustainable population.

Alaska Native organizations criticized the manner in which these determinations were to be undertaken, arguing that the model on which the "stock" assessments are founded is fundamentally flawed:

> Instead of an ecosystem approach, which takes into account the entire system, the stock assessments are based on a single species approach. . . . [Furthermore,] the stock assessments are based on what for some species is extremely limited, and in some cases non-existent, western scientific data. . . . The vast information (local science) that is locally held about all the species is not incorporated into the entire process. As a result, PBRs are potentially very dangerous: not only are they based on what in most cases is either non-existent, limited, or dated data, the PBRs also provide an absolute number which may then be used by certain groups unfriendly to Native interests as a limit on Native take.

Nevertheless, Alaska Natives became actively involved in the "stock" assessment process, and have the option of requesting adjudicatory hearings in the case of disputes involving any species used for subsistence.

A second 1994 MMPA amendment with direct bearing on management of beluga and other marine mammals is Section 119, which authorizes the Secretary of Commerce to ". . . *enter into cooperative agreements with Alaska Native organizations to conserve marine mammals and provide co-management of subsistence use by Alaska Natives.*" In Section 119, Congress also authorized expenditures up to $2.5 million annually between 1994 and 1999 for activities involving collecting and analyzing data on marine mammals, monitoring subsistence catches, participating in marine mammal research, and developing marine mammal comanagement structures. However, to date, only $250,000 has been appropriated for use under Section 119, and prospects for additional funding appear uncertain.

Alaska Native governments and organizations are building on this opportunity to expand marine mammal comanagement by developing both a process for using Section 119 funds and a model comanagement agreement with federal agencies for use as a possible template for future agreements. The Indigenous People's Council for Marine Mammals (IPCoMM), an umbrella coalition of Native marine mammal commissions and organizations (including the ABWC), is developing a strategy to identify appropriate indigenous organizations to participate in Section 119 comanagement agreements and to coordinate proposals to federal agencies for funding and negotiation of government-to-government agreements for management.

Current Beluga Whaling Management Issues in Alaska

As the previous section makes clear, the Section 119 amendment to the MMPA provides an important opportunity for building trust and cooperation between indigenous peoples and agencies in managing beluga and other marine mammals. With regard to beluga in Alaska, the ABWC has adopted its management plan but now seeks formal acceptance of the plan by Alaska Native governments, thereby enabling the ABWC to negotiate a specific beluga comanagement agreement with federal agencies under Section 119 of the MMPA.

A second management issue relates to concerns about Potential Biological Removal (PBR) determinations, and the adequacy of the available scientific data about beluga in Alaskan waters. Many hunters and Native organizations continue to have strong reservations about the validity of the PBRs and the process used to determine them. However, at present federal biologists believe that overall, the beluga population in Alaska is generally healthy. The one exception may be in Cook Inlet, where scientists estimate that there are about 1,200 beluga, and where the PBR for this "stock" would be no more than twenty-five to forty animals annually, which is less than the current take.

A third issue associated with management of beluga whales and whaling relates to the contribution of indigenous knowledge to both sustainable use of beluga and to Western resource management. Inuit and other indigenous people believe that indigenous knowledge must be fully considered in research and management of renewable resources.

A fourth management issue relates to concerns about industrial development within the range of beluga in Alaska, and to possible accumulation of contaminants in beluga tissue that might cause harm to humans. Consequently, the ABWC is involved in providing information about beluga ecology and behaviour to agencies and businesses involved in planning industrial development in coastal waters. In addition, ABWC has formally commented on specific development plans with a view to minimizing impacts of industrial activities on beluga, and is supporting studies designed to determine levels of contaminants in beluga.

Finally, beluga hunters are concerned about maintenance of an effective and appropriate beluga-management regime, for many fear that the IWC will seek to expand its control over small cetaceans (including beluga) in the coming years. At present, there is no consensus among IWC nations about the commission's competence to study and make management recommendations about small cetaceans. However, many nations represented in the IWC, including the United States, under strong pressure from whale preservation groups appear to favour such action. Inuit hunters believe strongly that it is inappropriate for the IWC to become involved in management of beluga and other small cetaceans, fearing the undue influence that antiwhaling groups have had, and continue to exert, over IWC affairs.

CANADA

Whaling by Canadian Inuit is managed at the present time under a number of separate legal agreements. In the case of Inuit in Nunavik (Northern Quebec), Nunavut (the eastern and central Canadian Arctic), and the Inuvialuit Settlement Region (the western Canadian Arctic), separate resource-management regimes, which involve whales and whaling, have been concluded with the Canadian government. Each of these separate agreements recognizes the constitutional rights of Canadian Inuit to hunt whales for subsistence purposes, a right that is guaranteed not only by the Canadian Constitution, but also by separate Acts of Parliament in each of the three cases. The Inuit of Labrador are only now entering into similar negotiations, and until an agreement is concluded, they hunt under the provisions of the Canada Fisheries Act, which allows Inuit to hunt whales for food, social, and ceremonial purposes (excepting certain species that are not hunted in Labrador at the present time).

The first of these political accords negotiated between the Canadian Inuit and the federal government was signed in 1975 (for Nunavik), followed by the Western Arctic Agreement (in 1984), and, most recently, the Nunavut Agreement (in 1993). Each of these agreements provides Inuit with increasing levels of guaranteed access to, and responsibility for, whales and whaling. Thus in the 1975 Nunavik agreement, certain levels of take by Inuit communities are guaranteed, at the level of take existing at the time the agreement was signed. The standing committee established under this agreement makes recommendations for changes to the federal Minister of Fisheries, who retains discretionary power to approve or disapprove the recommendations based on conservation considerations.

In the 1984 Western Arctic agreement, beneficiaries are guaranteed preferential access to all marine mammal species, with any permitted take that is surplus to community needs being available for commercial trade. The Fisheries Joint Management Committee (FJMC), a comanagement regime consisting of equal numbers of Inuit and government appointees, is empowered to make recommendations to the Minister on whaling matters. However, in this case, the Minister has severely limited discretionary powers to alter or reject FJMC recommendations.

Under the 1993 Nunavut agreement, the Nunavut Wildlife Management Board (NWMB), also a comanagement structure, determines existing levels of need, which also includes commercial uses. However, unlike the situation occurring under the two earlier agreements, the NWMB is empowered to make decisions that the Minister can only override on the basis of conservation or public safety concerns.

Another feature of these three agreements is the increasing extent of transfer of financial resources and administrative responsibility for research, from the federal government to the Inuit. A further difference exists between the first agreement, signed in 1975, and the two later agreements; in the 1975 agreement, marine waters are not expressly included in the agreement (because provincial–federal responsibilities were in dispute), though provisions for comanagement of whales and other marine mammals are included. However, at the present time further negotiations in connection with Quebec offshore waters are in progress, and it seems likely that attachments to the Nunavik agreement will bring it into conformity with the two later agreements.

Under the Western Arctic agreement, the Fisheries Joint Management Committee (FJMC) is responsible for establishing whale management plans. The beluga management plan, for example, has the goal of maintaining sustainable levels of take, of recommending and conducting research and monitoring (of hunts, whales, and the environment), and of developing educational programmes. This management plan is updated every three years, and contains bylaws and guidelines established by community level hunters' committees. Funding for such ongoing monitoring, research, and consultative activities is provided for under the terms of the 1984 agreement.

The Western Canadian Inuvialuit and the Alaskan Iñupiat hunt beluga from the same whale population, and for this reason attempts were made, in the early 1990s, to develop a joint management plan by forming the Alaska–Inuvialuit Beluga Whale Committee. However, given different approaches to whale management in the United States and Canada, at the present time it has not been possible to conclude a joint management agreement. However, recent research has adequately demonstrated that the levels of take by Iñupiat and Inuvialuit hunters from this large Western Arctic beluga population do not constitute a conservation issue. Under these favourable circumstances, an international management structure in the region is not seen as necessary at present, and a more informal exchange of information is considered an entirely appropriate arrangement.

Most years since 1991, when the first hunt in many years was carried out, the FJMC has also recommended that bowhead hunts take place; following these recommendations, licences have been issued on every occasion a request has been made. It is worth noting that under the terms of the Western Arctic agreement the Inuvialuit do not require a federal licence to hunt bowhead;

FIGURE 26. Although not required by law, in the spirit of cooperation, Inuvialuit bowhead hunters sign a federal whaling licence at Shingle Point, Canada, August 1991.

however, to foster a good cooperative relationship, the Inuvialuit do request a federal licence for each hunt.

Similarly, under the 1993 Nunavut agreement, provisions for resuming bowhead whaling in the eastern Canadian Arctic are specified, and a licence for a bowhead hunt was issued in 1996 and again in 1998. Under the terms of the Nunavut agreement, among the requirements for these hunts to be authorized was one mandating that a five-year Inuit traditional-knowledge study be undertaken, with funds provided under the terms of the Nunavut agreement. The Canadian government believes that these arrangements satisfactorily meet its legal obligations (under the whaling provisions of the Canadian Fisheries Act) to Inuit who are guaranteed the right to hunt for subsistence under the Canadian Constitution.

The Beaufort Sea Beluga Management Plan

In cooperation with hunters' and trappers' associations in the three principal Inuvialuit beluga-hunting communities (Aklavik, Inuvik, and Tuktoyaktuk), the Fisheries Joint Management Committee (FJMC) has developed a management plan for the beluga in the Canadian sector of the Beaufort Sea. The twin goals of this plan are to maintain a healthy population of beluga in the region, and to provide for optimum sustainable catches. In pursuit of these goals, a number of measures are taken to conserve beluga in the face of environmental changes, as well as to support other actions that may be necessary to ensure successful conduct of the plan.

Beluga hunting in the region is restricted to subsistence need and is entirely self-regulated. Generally, each household limits its catch to a single beluga, and females with calves are not taken. Indeed, hunting in the shallow waters off the Mackenzie Delta may be halted, even when beluga are abundant, whenever cloudy water-conditions prevent hunters from being completely certain that adult beluga are not accompanied by calves. Hunt monitors report catches at all whaling camps and collect biological data and specimens from the whales taken.

The superiority of self-regulation over imposing quotas is demonstrated by the near-constant level of hunting take, despite a rapidly increasing Inuvialuit population in the region over the past thirty years. Families are assured that they need not keep hunting each year simply to support an artificial need created by a quota system. Local families remain secure in the knowledge that the tradition of freely sharing mattak and meat continues in the absence of external pressures that create perceptions of threat to security of supply, and even of scarcity.

The Canadian Beaufort Sea has been an area of intense offshore oil and gas exploration, and shipping to resupply arctic coastal communities has long used the area as a logistics base. Thus, the management plan directly addresses questions of beluga habitat protection and mitigation of potential adverse impacts on beluga. This is done by establishing four management zones: (1) actual and potential beluga-hunting areas, (2) inshore (Mackenzie Delta and Tuktoyaktuk Peninsula), (3) offshore areas (Beaufort Sea), and (4) foreign and international waters. Guidelines are developed for each region to assist decision-makers, from the community to the national level, in becoming aware of special or international regulations, codes of conduct, and other considerations affecting beluga conservation and habitat, as well as to ensure that hunting and other compatible uses of beluga are not compromised.

Research and monitoring of both live beluga and the catch provides information with which to evaluate the soundness of the management plan and its implementation, and the consequent health of the beluga. A number of research studies have been carried out, including population assessments (which have resulted in a significant upward revision of beluga population estimates) and a study of Inuvialuit traditional knowledge concerning beluga. The Inuvialuit are involved in all phases of these research and monitoring activities. The plan has also initiated school and hunter education programmes.

Canada and the IWC

Canada, a founding member of the International Whaling Commission, left the organization in 1982. The federal government recognizes that bowhead are the one species of whale hunted in Canada that fall under IWC management. However, Canada asserts that authorizing bowhead hunting under the terms of the land claim agreements does not require rejoining the IWC. The UN Convention of the Law of the Sea (UNCLOS) only obliges countries to *"work through the appropriate international organizations"* for the conservation, management, and study of whales. Thus, UNCLOS does not require countries to "join" an international organization (by becoming a member), but rather states that it is sufficient for a country to "work through" the appropriate organizations (plural); the use of the plural clearly implies that the IWC is not being specifically named as *the* organization. In Canada's view, that nation works through the IWC, by providing the IWC Scientific Committee with timely information on whales and whaling activities in its waters, and also by having Canadian scientists periodically participate in meetings of the IWC Scientific Committee. Canada also sends a Government Observer delegation to IWC meetings, and on occasion has been invited to address the meetings.

In the Canadian whaling context, the IWC is not considered an "appropriate" organization. The Canadian Inuit have attended IWC meetings in the past, and subsequently passed a number of resolutions at their own annual general assemblies that make it quite clear they do not consider IWC behaviour acceptable. For example, their General Assembly Resolutions 92-9 (in 1992), and 93-4 (in 1993) point out that *"current and proposed activities at the IWC with respect to the management of small cetaceans would compromise the constitutionally protected harvesting rights of Canadian Inuit . . . "* and *"the current trend within the IWC is inconsistent with resource management based on sustainable use principles. . . ."* A resolution passed by the Legislative Assembly of the Northwest Territories in March 1992 condemned actions of the IWC, which it claimed *"is dominated by member nations that pursue a goal of irrational protectionism rather than management of whale stocks,"* and made it clear that the Legislative Assembly joined with Canadian Inuit organizations in opposing Canada's membership in the IWC. Inuit students from across Nunavut, participating in the Nunavut Sivuniksavut public administration training programme in Ottawa, researched the whaling issue in April 1995, and concluded:

> Given the reality of the structure of IWC and the motivation of some of its members [we] felt that there would be no justification for the Commission to take on the primary responsibility for managing the smaller whales. In fact, in [our] minds there doesn't appear to be justification for very much of what the IWC was up to in terms of management of any whales.

In a February 1994 letter addressed to the Ministers of Fisheries and Oceans, Environment, Foreign Affairs and International Trade, and Indian and Northern Affairs (with copies to parliamentarians and the Premier of the Northwest Territories), the President of Inuit Tapirisat of Canada reminded the Ministers that, with regard to the three Inuit land claim agreements concluded with Canada, the hunting and game management provisions are among the most important parts of these agreements. Her letter continued *"The IWC does not appear to be capable of any assistance in [the management] area . . . [as] it has become dominated by a protectionist anti-hunting sentiment, and has lost any hope of instituting a rational or scientific whale management regime. . . . Inuit see the IWC as an obstacle, not an aid, to effective management of whale stocks."* The letter reminded Ministers of the role Inuit are legally required to play in reaching future decisions that may affect their constitutionally and legally guaranteed hunting rights under their land claim agreements, and concludes that *"for Canada to rejoin the IWC would be a grave error."*

In a reply to this February letter, the Canadian Minister of Fisheries and Oceans assured the Inuit national leader that any decisions on whaling issues affecting the Inuit will only be taken in accordance with the requirements and the spirit of their land claim agreements. The Minister also stated: *"It has been longstanding Canadian policy not to be a member of the IWC, and that continues to be the position of my department."*

The Canadian Inuit continue stressing to the Canadian government their opposition to future membership in the IWC, with the reasons for their opposition confirmed by decisions taken each year by the IWC, as well as by the increasingly antiwhaling sentiments expressed by various IWC member governments. In September 1994, representatives of all Inuit regional organizations met in Ottawa to discuss whaling. In a letter to federal Ministers after that meeting, the Inuit national president stated that *"barring a drastic (and highly unlikely) re-alignment of the priorities and the very functioning of the IWC, that body remains in our view a disastrously inappropriate vehicle for marine mammal management."* Continuing meetings between Inuit and government officials to discuss whaling matters (such as in September and November 1996) have reaffirmed this position. IWC Resolution 1996-9, opposing the 1996 Canadian bowhead hunts, followed by the United States's initiating a process of certification that could lead to trade sanctions against Canada, appears to have made the question of Canadian membership in the IWC no longer a matter for serious discussion in Canada: in a CBC radio interview (September 13, 1996) a senior official of the federal Fisheries and Oceans department, in answer to a question, stated: *"We have no intention of joining the International Whaling Commission."*

The Southeast Baffin Beluga Managment Plan

In March 1990, the Canadian Department of Fisheries and Oceans (DFO) set new beluga quotas for Pangnirtung, Iqaluit, and Lake Harbour (Kimmirut) in the southeast Baffin region. This action resulted because federal scientists had decided that, in their opinion, the three communities were taking an unsustainable number of whales from a single, severely depleted, beluga population, which consequently would become extinct in a few years. The scientists advised that there should be no hunting allowed for a ten-year period; however, the Minister of Fisheries, recognizing the cultural importance of beluga to Inuit in the region, allowed a small interim quota of five beluga per year for each community.

Local opposition to the new quotas was immediate and intense. The quotas were described as "a cruel act against the communities," and the anguish felt by many hunters was likened to "the grief associated with losing a loved one." Inuit hunters expressed fear that they would not be able to pass on their hunting traditions to their children; quotas were considered a violation of Inuit rights, and protests were held in the three affected communities. Following representation from Inuit and territorial government politicians, quotas were increased to about thirty-five beluga for each community—on the condition that hunters work with federal government scientists to conduct new surveys and prepare a comanagement plan to conserve local beluga.

A committee, composed of government personnel and Inuit hunters, met to consider the many disagreements existing between local knowledge and scientists' knowledge. An early decision was that quotas should be set independently for each Inuit community. A new spirit of cooperation and shared responsibility developed, and continued, as local hunter organizations managed the whale hunts with the assistance of DFO personnel. In this connection, hunters submitted biological samples for analysis, and clifftop surveys were jointly conducted in order to begin making assessments of annual changes in beluga numbers.

Significant progress in resolving these different interpretations of beluga population status was not made until there was mutual recognition that the nature of these disagreements was based on cultural conflicts. These conflicts involved not only different understandings of the perceived "facts" that government scientists and hunters possessed, but also different interpretations of the meaning and significance of these different "facts."

Significant progress was finally made when the Inuit and government officials agreed that the common goal of the committee should be to manage and conserve the traditional relationship existing between Inuit and beluga in the southeast Baffin region. This was a significant step forward, for now the basic management unit is no longer the contentious "stock" of beluga, but rather the relationship between the resource users and the resource. It was also agreed that both parties could bring different types of knowledge and insight to the discussions. The foundations were being laid for true comanagement; Inuit on the committee did not have to think like biologists nor accept the state management model, and biologists did not have to adopt an Inuit cultural perspective nor adopt local management styles and philosophies.

This comanagement plan, prepared by Inuit and federal fisheries department personnel to resolve the southeast Baffin beluga controversy, was accepted by the Minister of Fisheries in 1994, and by the NWMB in 1995. The plan represents a compromise by both parties, for each achieved less than they had wanted, but more than would likely have been received if a comanagement plan had not been produced. Although the plan has yet to be implemented, it points the way for the establishment of true resource comanagement regimes in Nunavut.

Cultural Conflicts Impeding a Solution

Both Inuit and federal officials agreed that fewer beluga were present in Cumberland Sound than occurred previously. However, the reasons for this decrease in numbers remained in dispute. Biologists claimed that commercial whaling, followed by years of intensive subsistence hunting, had decimated this local "stock," while Inuit maintained that beluga had become more dispersed because of increased local boat ownership and use during the 1970s, the stranding of the resident pod of killer whales in 1978, and the disappearance of the dominant beluga in Cumberland Sound sometime in the late 1960s.

The latter explanation is especially poignant, as it underscores the integrity and value of local management systems and the traditional ecological knowledge that informs these systems. Inuit living in camps around the head of Cumberland Sound were always instructed never to hunt a particular whale they called Luuq, as this whale was the one that other beluga followed into Clearwater Fiord. They also knew that if Luuq was killed beluga would no longer travel or concentrate in large numbers. Although the connection between the disappearance of Luuq and the nonselective netting of more than 120 beluga by a biologist for scientific purposes in 1966–1967 has not been established, after Luuq's disappearance beluga in Cumberland Sound became more dispersed and difficult to hunt.

Inuit and federal officials also disagreed over certain other issues. While biologists determined the precommercial exploitation size of the southeast Baffin beluga "stock" to be more than 5,000, Inuit stated that they had never before seen such numbers of beluga at one time or place, not even in Clearwater Fiord (where the largest summering populations occur). A review of the Hudson's Bay Company Pangnirtung trading-post journals supported Inuit claims: the single largest whale drive ever recorded produced no more than 500 animals—a number not substantially different than what can be seen in the area today. Supporting Inuit assertions that the beluga population had not declined significantly was the fact that the number of whales observed in 1990 (more than 500) was even larger than that counted in 1986 (less than 500), despite the fact that some 400 beluga were taken during the intervening period.

After acknowledging that some problems may exist with their numbers, federal scientists expressed concern that there were far too few breeding females in the "stock," and that it would soon be driven to extinction if the Inuit did not stop hunting adult females. However, Inuit reminded the biologists that they had been actively avoiding hunting adults with calves (that is to say, adult females) for years, and therefore the samples they were providing did not reflect the actual structure of the population, and would, of course, be deficient in female beluga. A similar misunderstanding arose when biologists expressed concerns about the lack of adult male beluga in the samples they were getting. Again, they were told that Inuit hunters do not normally kill adult male beluga because they are much more difficult to hunt, and that the sample (composed largely of young males) was therefore not at all representative of the population.

While the biologists preferred to view whales in the southeast Baffin region as belonging to a "stock" or "stocks," which could then be "managed" as "management units," Inuit on the committee said that they would be ashamed to think they could *manage* animals, for only God can do that. There are no concepts in Inuttitut for a group of animals that includes individuals beyond one's field of vision. The concept of "stock" was seen to be irrelevant and arbitrary, as were other concepts and terms that lie at the heart of the biologists' management model, such as "management," "harvest," and "wildlife." Some Inuit even dislike the term "conservationist" applied to them, as they do not possess a conservation ethic in the sense that the concept is understood and used by environmentalists living in southern Canada or the conservation bureaucracy. Rather, the Inuit use of animals is governed by a profound respect for a partnership with animals, as well as the principle of least effort when taking animals for the needed products they provide. This relationship does not include the need to conserve what is left just because some animals have necessarily been used.

GREENLAND

Whaling in Greenland is managed by the Home Rule Government in cooperation with local municipalities, the Greenland Hunters' and Fishermen's Association (KNAPK), and the Association of Greenland Municipalities (KANUKOKA). In the case of the larger whale species (such as minke and fin whales), the Home Rule enacts laws and regulations in accordance with IWC quotas and guidelines. In 1995, the quota for West Greenland was 155 minke whales and 19 fin whales. In East Greenland, the quota was 12 minke whales. For narwhal and beluga, management is based on advice provided by the Canada–Greenland Joint Commission on the Conservation and Management of Narwhal and Beluga. Greenland is also a member of the North Atlantic Marine Mammal Commission (NAMMCO).

Since the advent of Home Rule in 1979, Greenland has developed an increasingly effective whaling management regime. Today, the regime is based on a combination of hunters' knowledge and advice from biologists as well as others in the scientific community. As Greenland's Minister of Fisheries and Industry recently stated:

In Greenland we . . . have to make a constant effort to ensure that our hunting meets standards of sustainable utilization. . . . Greenland works domestically for:

- The best possible distribution and utilization of hunting potential

- As accurate reporting of catches as possible

- The necessary resources [being] made available for the development and improvement of hunting equipment

- Intervention if hunting regulations are infringed

- The necessary resources made available for biological research

The quotas for minke and fin whales are allocated to municipalities in consultation with KNAPK and KANUKOKA based on a number of considerations. These factors include community population, the availability of fishing vessels equipped with harpoon cannons, the availability of alternative resources within the community, and the number of smaller settlements within a municipality. Once quotas are allocated, municipalities work with local hunters' and fishers' associations to determine which hunters will receive a whaling permit. Among other requirements, Home Rule regulations specify that minke and fin whales must be taken by fishing vessels equipped with harpoon cannons of 50 mm or larger calibre using the penthrite grenade. Where this equipment is not available (particularly in smaller settlements), hunters can receive special permission from the Home Rule government to take minke whales in collective hunts, where hunters in outboard motor–powered skiffs use rifles and float-equipped harpoons to kill and retrieve the whales.

Hunters taking minke and fin whales are required to have a whaling licence, and must report details of their catch or strike to municipal and Home Rule authorities. Biological samples are also required to be provided to the appropriate authorities. Violation of regulations results in confiscation of the products, and may lead to reduction in the entire community's whaling quota the following year.

In the case of beluga and narwhal regulations, these are enacted by the Home Rule government and local municipalities based on management advice received from the Canada–Greenland Joint Commission. Recently, following advice from the Joint Commission, Greenland has enacted new regulations that prohibit the taking of beluga by hunters in larger vessels, and that place a restriction on the numbers of beluga that can be taken by those hunting from smaller vessels. Since 1995, beluga drives have also been prohibited.

Current Whaling Management Issues in Greenland

Greenland continues to refine and improve its whaling management by utilizing the knowledge of Inuit hunters and the best advice of biologists and other scientists. However, hunters continue to face a number of challenges in promoting sustainable use of whales and other marine mammals. Foremost among these is opposition to whaling from animal protection organizations that are ideologically opposed to the taking of any whales. Many hunters in Greenland believe the IWC is dominated by such views, and consequently they adamantly oppose the suggestion that IWC should extend its jurisdiction to include small cetaceans, fearing that rational discussion and management would be impossible in such a forum.

Related to such concerns are discussions at the IWC and in other fora that oppose the sale of whale products within Greenland. To some antiwhaling groups and government members of IWC, the sale of whale products (which has long existed in Greenland) constitutes a "commercial" hunt, which should be forbidden to aboriginal hunters under IWC rules. However, to Greenlanders, such local sales are entirely consistent with the goals of sustainable community development and with the cultural goals of ensuring that customary food is widely distributed to those who need to eat it. Thus, if properly managed, these exchanges sustain and promote both a high level of local self-sufficiency and Inuit cultural values as well.

Greenlanders also face challenges over the use of new technologies. In the IWC, some opponents of whaling argue that Inuit whalers are no longer "real" hunters (and thus entitled to continue subsistence hunting) if they use modern equipment. At the same time, whalers are criticized if they do not use the most modern equipment to address issues raised in discussions about "humane killing." Inuit have no permanent attachment to "traditional" technology: kayaks, harpoons, and dog teams survive because under certain circumstances there are no better alternatives; however, it is many centuries of technological innovation that have ensured Inuit survival in a demanding and changing environment, and such changes continue to be made today.

RUSSIA

The situation faced by native whalers in Russia is in stark contrast to that of Inuit whalers in Alaska, Canada, and Greenland. After many decades of having been denied a meaningful role in whaling management discussions by the authorities of the former Soviet Union, they find their situation further confounded today by a lack of resources that would enable them to organize regionally and to engage meaningfully in dialogue with the current Russian federal authorities.

From 1969 until 1992, the national government operated a large catcher-boat whaling operation (using a non-native crew) to catch mainly gray whales, which were then delivered to some ten to twelve native coastal communities. This vessel was operated by the Ministry of Fisheries, while the allocation of the IWC quota of gray whales to the villages fell under the authority of a different department of government, namely the Directorate of State Farms of the Chukotka Autonomous Region. Village quotas were normally set according to the size of local fox farms, beach conditions for landing and processing whales, and the availability of alternate food supplies for the farmed foxes. Thus, quotas could vary for similar-sized communities, from zero to twenty-five whales for different communities each having about 400 residents. The town of Lorino, with some 1,000 native residents, usually received about half of the annual quota, or between seventy and eighty gray whales.

Native people could do little to influence the village quotas or participate in any aspects of managing the hunts. However, the system guaranteed an annual supply of free, or very inexpensive, fresh local food to the majority of communities. Despite the nontraditional manner of hunting (including non-participation of local hunters), nevertheless the distribution and consumption of the whale followed traditional norms of sharing and cooperation, and kept alive certain practices and also an appreciation of the whale-based diet and the importance of whales to the local society.

After 1992, the catcher-boat whaling operation ceased, and local hunters in several villages immediately began to resume community-based whaling using small wood and skin boats, rifles, hand-held spears, and harpoons with floats. The IWC-imposed quota (140 gray whales per year for the past several years, but reduced to an average of 120 per year for the period 1998–2002) is distributed among the villages and state farms, and, as the skill level increases, the number of whales taken is also increasing, though it remains well within the limit set by the quota. At the present time, a new Ministry of Environmental Affairs has taken over international representation and IWC negotiations from the Ministry of Fisheries, though the latter agency continues to monitor all sea-mammal hunting in Russian waters.

Chukotkan native sea-mammal hunters have been involved, since 1980, with Russian sea-mammal research projects, and in more recent years, through their participation in ICC meetings and contacts with Alaskan whalers, they have gained more understanding of the international dimensions of whaling politics and regulation.

The current situation among Chukotka whalers is discussed earlier in this book; here it is noted that the marine-mammal hunters of Chukotka hope to organize themselves to assume a greater role in managing their relationship to the whales on which, to such a great extent, their culture and community economies depend. Thus, in 1995, at a meeting with Alaskan whalers in Barrow, a Chukotkan native delegation, which included hunters and political

FIGURE 27. All are welcome to help themselves to mattak when a whale is landed. Sireniki, Chukotka, 1985.

leaders from several communities, made a formal request for assistance in their efforts to resume community-based whaling, with training and equipment being the most urgent forms of assistance requested from the Alaskans. The Alaskans have responded with whaling guns, outboard motors, and other needed equipment, together with useful joint bowhead research studies. In addition, the ICC, with funds made available from the Canadian International Development Agency and the Greenland Home Rule Government, are also assisting the Chukotkan communities to increase their involvement in international meetings, such as the IWC and the World Council of Whalers.

A relatively new issue beginning to be addressed now is the extent to which Chukotkan and Alaskan hunters both hunt from the same population of bowhead whales. Hunters on St. Lawrence Island and in Chukotkan villages have long said that some bowheads migrating through the Bering Strait swim westward and spend much of their time in the Arctic Ocean north of Chukotka. As far back as 1982 and 1983, Russian representatives to the IWC requested a small take of bowheads for indigenous peoples on the Chukchi Peninsula. This request was repeated in 1988 and as recently as 1996, when, on failing to receive a quota from the IWC, the Russian authorities issued a licence in the fall of 1996 for two bowheads to be taken by native whalers.

The AEWC has developed a cooperative "Alaska–Chukotka Program for Encouragement of Native Involvement in Policy and Decision Processes" with people in Chukotka. This includes cooperation in conducting surveys of bowhead whales in the region, because

> We know from what our grandfathers and great-grandfathers told our parents that a whale stock exists in the Russian waters. In terms of the size of the population, we don't know. [But] an agreement has been entered into under Mayor Ahmaogak's administration with the Russian Yuit [Yup'iit] to monitor and do a census [of the] whale population. [This] will help in providing sound scientific knowledge to the scientific community as to the real status of the bowhead whale stock.
>
> *Delbert Rexford, Barrow, April 1995*

Using funding initially from the North Slope Borough, more than forty people from Chukotkan communities are now involved in doing survey work related to bowheads. Preliminary results show that there are at least several hundred bowhead whales in the region during summer months. Russian scientists report bowhead sightings during the summer months from the Bering Strait westward to the Kara Sea and the Kola Peninsula. Other studies are using genetic techniques to determine relationships between whales found near

Chukotka and those taken in Alaska. If people in Chukotka begin to regularly take bowhead, it may well have implications for Alaskan hunters. What those implications might be is difficult to say, but clearly Alaskan and Chukotkan hunters are actively sharing information and resources to learn more about these whales and to support sustainable whaling practices. To this end, the Chukotkan whalers seek to establish a Chukotkan Whaling Commission, with an initial goal of increasing the cooperation between Inuit whaling captains in both Alaska and Chukotka.

CANADA—GREENLAND JOINT COMMISSION ON NARWHAL AND BELUGA

The Canada–Greenland Joint Commission on the Conservation and Management of Narwhal and Beluga was formed to address common management and conservation issues concerning the use of narwhal and beluga *that are believed to migrate* between Greenlandic and Canadian waters (emphasis added, as recent tagging studies cast doubt on the assumption that Canada and Greenland share a common "stock"). The commission was established in 1991 under a Memorandum of Understanding (MOU) between the Canadian Department of Fisheries and Oceans and the Greenland Home Rule Government's Ministry of Fisheries, Hunting, and Agriculture. The MOU recognizes the importance of narwhal and beluga hunting to Inuit communities in both countries, and notes the concern of both governments for *"the rational management, conservation and optimum utilization of living resources of the sea"* as reflected in the 1982 UN Convention on the Law of the Sea. Canada and Greenland each have two co-commissioners, one representing the government, the other the hunter community. Delegations include hunters' organizations and members of comanagement bodies, such as the Greenland Hunters and Fishers Organization (KNAPK) and the Nunavut Wildlife Management Board. Frequently, hunters representing communities that depend on either or both species of whale are also invited to participate in the meetings of the commission.

Major activities of the commission are undertaken by the Scientific Working Group (SWG). Composed largely of fisheries scientists and whale biologists, the SWG has concluded that the number of beluga wintering off West Greenland has declined significantly since 1981, and that the present take (approximately 770 per year by Greenlandic and Canadian hunters) is unsustainable. A roughly similar number of narwhal are taken by Inuit on both sides of Baffin

Bay, but in this case the take is considered sustainable and the narwhal population is not being overexploited. Studies have been undertaken to determine the status of whale "stocks" (through aerial surveys), "stock" identity (through genetic and other means), and the analysis of catch statistics.

Although the conclusions and recommendations of the SWG to date have been largely based on western scientific studies, the Commission is attempting to include the traditional ecological knowledge (TEK) of hunters in the deliberations of the SWG. Disagreements between biologists' and Greenlandic hunters' assessments of some issues are acute, as in the case of the disputed status of beluga populations in West Greenland. Hunters find their own observations on beluga numbers in serious disagreement with the alarming conclusions reached by scientists, and they report seeing many beluga offshore. Hunters cite increased ship traffic (both commercial fishing and general shipping) and fluctuations in food supply as causes of change in the migration patterns and distribution of beluga, and thus the progressive reduction in numbers of beluga counted in West Greenland coastal waters. Although the SWG has commissioned TEK studies to address beluga reproduction and changes in migration patterns, these studies are framed within a scientific paradigm and seek answers to problems identified by scientists, and by methods that appear reasonable to scientists. The broader context in which Inuit TEK derives its meaning and value is not being considered. Moreover, attempts to quantify this knowledge serve to devalue and decontextualize it, thus undermining its efficacy and potential contribution to comanagement.

At present, neither Inuit nor the Joint Commission have any specific concerns about the status of the shared narwhal population. In fact, on the basis of completed studies, the Joint Commission has concluded that present takes of narwhal in the region appear to be sustainable. While further studies have been recommended, the high struck-and-lost rate that has always been associated with narwhal hunting—for, unlike beluga, narwhal are not usually found in shallow waters—remains an issue that Inuit are attempting to address. Indeed, some hunters from Broughton Island take considerable pride in the fact that they now harpoon narwhal before shooting them.

The strengths of the Canada–Greenland Joint Commission are that it employs a regional approach, deals exclusively with Inuit-hunted small cetaceans, supports sustainable use, and is sensitive to Inuit concerns. However, restricting the scope of this Joint Commission to these two whale species may be questionable from an ecological and management perspective, where knowledge of other utilized species of marine mammals is potentially important for an appropriate understanding of beluga and narwhal interactions with hunters. Thus, some major challenges facing the Commission, and the SWG in particular, will be to find ways (1) to expand the Commission's mandate and authority, and (2) to meaningfully incorporate Inuit expertise and knowledge into decision-making and management actions.

THE NORTH ATLANTIC MARINE MAMMAL COMMISSION

In April 1992, Greenland, the Faroe Islands, Iceland, and Norway signed an agreement in Nuuk, Greenland, thereby establishing the North Atlantic Marine Mammal Commission (NAMMCO). The groundwork for establishing this organization was laid during a meeting in Reykjavik, Iceland in 1988 attended by government representatives of the four NAMMCO countries together with government observers from Canada, Japan, and Russia. Following this meeting, the North Atlantic Committee for Cooperation on Research on Marine Mammals was created in 1990, leading to the signing of the NAMMCO agreement in 1992.

The aim of this international commission is to strengthen cooperation for the conservation, study, management, and rational utilization of marine mammals in the North Atlantic region. The Commission seeks to do this through utilizing the best scientific information, including a thorough understanding of the complexity of the marine ecosystem, and considering the rights and needs of coastal communities to make a sustainable living from marine living resources. The Preamble to the NAMMCO Agreement states that the parties to the agreement are as one in

> Having regard to their common concerns for the rational management, conservation, and optimum utilization of the living resources of the sea in accordance with generally accepted principles of international law . . . [and are] . . .
>
> Convinced that regional bodies in the North Atlantic can ensure effective conservation, sustainable marine resource utilization and development with due regard to the needs of coastal communities and indigenous people.

The NAMMCO has a Council (the decision-making body) that meets annually. A Scientific Committee provides scientific advice to the Council, and a Management Committee recommends management and scientific actions to the Council. In the immediate past, the Scientific Committee has provided advice on pilot whales, killer whales, and northern bottlenose whales (as well as on walrus and on ringed, harp, grey, and hooded seals). From time to time, ad hoc groups are established to deal with specific matters that may arise, such as developing technical advice on hunting methods or planning observer schemes for coastal whaling operations. There is a Secretariat in Tromsø, Norway, as well as the NAMMCO Fund, established to assist in disseminating knowledge and understanding about marine-mammal conservation and sustainable use.

NAMMCO follows an ecosystem, or multispecies, approach to its assessment of marine resource issues. A recent initiative was to convene an international conference to examine both the sources, levels, and effects of organochlorine and heavy-metal pollutants on the marine ecosystem and the social, economic, and health consequences for those people whose diet is at risk of being contaminated. A recent multivessel (and aircraft) regional initiative was the 1995 North Atlantic cetacean sighting survey, to assess the distribution and abundance of North Atlantic whale populations. In 1997, a major international conference on seals and sealing was held.

As an international organization, NAMMCO exchanges information and cooperates with a number of other relevant international bodies, such as the International Council for the Exploration of the Sea (ICES), the Northwest Atlantic Fisheries Organization (NAFO), the IWC, the UN Food and Agriculture Organization (FAO), and so on. The Greenland Home Rule government is a full member of NAMMCO and, at the present time, Canada has Government Observer status and is reviewing the extent of its future involvement. Also at the present time, Canada cooperates fully with the NAMMCO Scientific Committee. The Greenland Hunters and Fishers Organization (KNAPK) is represented on the Greenland delegation at NAMMCO meetings, and the Inuvialuit Game Council attends meetings as nongovernmental observers. Some members of NAMMCO see it as satisfying UN Convention of the Law of the Sea (UNCLOS) requirements for the management of whale species occurring in its geographic area of management responsibility:

> With reference to the larger whales—minke, fin, and humpback whales—that KNAPK prioritizes for hunting, these populations are North Atlantic populations. KNAPK believes that these should be considered in conjunction with nearby countries, the nearest neighbours—Canada, Iceland, Norway and the Faroes, and possibly Russia. The Rio Declaration has given us the opportunity for regional management of marine mammals. . . . Since the start of NAMMCO, KNAPK has sought, and continues to hope, that the decision-making process with reference to the larger whales also be included in NAMMCO's work.
>
> *Anton Siegstad and Hansi Kreutzmann, Nuuk, May 1995*

In a letter to the Canadian Ministers of Fisheries and Oceans, Foreign Affairs, Environment, and Indian and Northern Affairs, the President of Inuit Tapirisat of Canada wrote:

> The establishment of the North Atlantic Marine Mammal Commission (NAMMCO) is another important development. We believe that NAMMCO represents a good start at addressing the needs for regional management of whale stocks. The states that share the whale stocks need to share responsibility for their management. This is precisely what structures like NAMMCO are set up to do. . . . I would urge Canada to take up full membership responsibilities in NAMMCO.
>
> *Rosemarie Kuptana, letter dated February 23, 1994*

Similar urging of the Canadian government by the Canadian Inuit has continued, at various regional and national meetings. At one such meeting, in November 1996, attended by a representative of NAMMCO, the four Canadian Inuit regional organizations (from Nunavut, the Inuvialuit Settlement Region [Western Arctic], Nunavik [Northern Quebec], and Labrador, respectively) reaffirmed their unanimous position that Canada should become a full member of NAMMCO. A 1998 report by the all-party Canadian Parliamentary Standing Committee on Foreign Affairs also strongly endorsed the view that Canada become a full member of NAMMCO.

SUGGESTED READINGS

Adams, M., K. J. Frost, and L. A. Harwood. 1993. Alaska and Inuvialuit Beluga Whale Committee (AIBWC): An initiative in "at home management." *Arctic* 46(2):134–37.

Alaska Consultants and S. R. Braund & Associates. 1984. *Subsistence Study of Alaska Eskimo Whaling Villages*. Anchorage, Alaska.

Alaska Native Review Commission. 1984. Transcript of Proceedings, Roundtable Discussions Volume XVI, Subsistence. Oct. 11, 1984.

Braund, S. R., S. W. Stoker, and J. A. Kruse. 1988. *Quantification of Subsistence and Cultural Need for Bowhead Whales by Alaska Eskimos*. Document TC/40/AS2. Cambridge, England: International Whaling Commission.

Caulfield, R. A. 1997. *Greenlanders, Whales and Whaling: Sustainability and Self-Determination in the Arctic*. Hanover, NH, and London: University Press of New England.

Fisheries Joint Management Committee. *Beaufort Sea Beluga Management Plan.* (Available from: Joint Secretariat, P.O. Box 2120, Inuvik, NWT, Canada, XOE OTO).

Freeman, M. M. R. 1989. The Alaska Eskimo Whaling Commission: successful co-management under extreme conditions. In: E. Pinkerton (ed.), *Cooperative Management of Local Fisheries: New Directions for Improved Management and Community-development*, pp. 137–53. Vancouver: University of British Columbia Press.

Goodman, D. 1997. Inuit land claim agreements and the management of whaling in the Canadian Arctic. In: H. Okada (ed.), *11th International Symposium on Peoples and Cultures of the North*. Abashiri, Japan: Hokkaido Museum of Northern Peoples.

Hazard, K. 1988. Beluga whale. In: J. W. Lentfer (ed.), *Selected Marine Mammals in Alaska: Species Accounts with Research and Management Recommendations*. Washington, D.C.: Marine Mammal Commission.

Hoel, A. H. 1993. Regionalization of international whale management: The case of the North Atlantic Marine Mammal Commission. *Arctic* 46(2):116–23.

Huntington, H. P., and Nikolai I. Mymrin (eds.). 1996. *Traditional Ecological Knowledge of Beluga Whales: An Indigenous Knowledge Pilot Project in the Chukchi and Northern Bering Seas*. Anchorage, Alaska: Inuit Circumpolar Conference.

Planning Committee for the Co-management of Southeast Baffin Beluga. 1994. *Co-management Plan for Southeast Baffin Beluga*. Prepared for the Department of Fisheries and Oceans and Nunavut Wildlife Management Board. (Available from the NWMB, P.O. Box 1379, Iqaluit, NWT, Canada, XOA OHO.)

Wheeler, P. 1995. The 1994 MMPA amendments: How will they effect the Native community? *Alaska Marine Resources* 8(1):2–3.

CHAPTER FIVE

Challenges to the
Sustainable Use of Whales by Inuit

THE QUESTION OF SUSTAINABILITY

In 1995, the Canadian National Round Table on Environment and Economy reported:

> If sustainable development succeeds, it will be because we have adjusted our value system. It will be because we have extended our measure of worth and because we have placed the concept of well-being at the centre of our considerations.

The issue of competing value systems is indeed the greatest challenge to Inuit use of local resources. It is fashionable in some circles to claim that whales, being migratory, are part of "the common heritage of humankind" and therefore are everyone's whales. Indeed, it is entirely reasonable to believe that the genetic resources of the entire biosphere are similarly part of the global heritage of all peoples, and it is for that reason that international resource-management agreements are entered into by many nations on behalf of their citizens.

However, such international conventions generally recognize the need of people to utilize the biological resources to satisfy such human needs as food and economic security. As the Canadian National Round Table Report on Environment and Economy observed:

> At the heart of sustainable development is the holistic perception that the well-being of people depends on the well-being of all other parts of our world—and that means the well-being of the ecosystem, the well-being of our economic system, the well-being of our institutions, and the well-being of societies.

With that understanding, the purpose of international resource management agreements has been to ensure that resource use is sustainable. For example, the preamble to the 1992 Convention on Biological Diversity states that governments are *"determined to conserve and sustainably use biological diversity for the benefit of present and future generations."* The reference to future generations clearly implies sustainability of resource use. The International Convention for the Regulation of Whaling conformed to that sense of obligation to ongoing resource use practices when it established its goal to *"provide for the proper conservation of whales and thus make possible the orderly development of the whaling industry."*

Whaling peoples in the modern world, however, confront a number of threats to their security, including the collective threat posed by numbers of people who are ideologically opposed to the human use of animals. Whalers, therefore, now experience the same opposition that over the years has also been faced by various others using animals in ways deemed unacceptable by animal protectionists. These others include sealers, trappers, furriers, medical researchers, and, more recently, zoological park operators, circus promoters, meat retailers, and even restaurateurs whose premises display live lobsters.

However, in the case of whaling the opposition is more organized, and more determined—perhaps because whales, like dinosaurs and elephants, are huge. Their size inspires awe: to many people, they are regarded as "uniquely special." Of course, all whale species *are* unique, as is every other animal species. However, extending the belief in the uniqueness of whales through to according them special rights not enjoyed by other food species poses a problem, both in law and in morality. Laws and regulations do exist to ensure that whales are conserved and that their use is legitimate according to the recognized legal norms and social practices of whale-using nations. However, such internationally accepted bases of legitimacy are disregarded by opponents of whaling, and such legal safeguards mean little against the zeal and dogmatism of believers in whale sanctity who occupy positions of authority in, for example, Washington, D.C., London, Brussels, and Bonn.

Can whales be used sustainably? There certainly is no scientific justification for our believing that whales are any different from other living creatures, whose natural increase allows use of some portion of their annual population increase without damaging the ability of the population to maintain itself. In a strictly rational, or scientific, sense, there can be no disputing such a conclusion.

However, many decisions about resource use have become highly politicized, and therefore are not entirely rational or science-based. Indeed, for certain wildlife species (including whales and other "charismatic" animal species, such as elephants), decisions respecting use of these resources are no longer made on a strictly scientific basis by some governments. Thus, in the sections to follow, the question of sustainable resource use is discussed further, and more especially the impediments to such use, as well as measures that can be taken to enhance the sustainability of that use.

ARCTIC POLLUTION AND CONTAMINATION

If we are to take our scientific advisers seriously, general pollution by heavy metals, pesticides, PCBs, and dioxin will assume dangerous levels in the years to come. . . . The closer the animals are to the top of the food chain, the more serious is the problem. We also cannot afford to ignore completely the warnings from some specialists that . . . sea mammals may simply become so polluted that they will be unfit for human consumption. . . . For us, the fact remains that only a meat-eater can live in symbiosis with Arctic nature. . . . Different peoples, different climates, different diets.

Finn Lynge, in Arctic Wars: Animal Rights, Endangered Peoples, *1992*

Today, the rights and capacity of Inuit to use whales in a sustainable manner are being challenged in many ways. The chemical pollution of Arctic and subarctic waters by industrial contamination represents a threat that deeply concerns many Inuit. Many areas of the Arctic now contain relatively high levels of PCBs and other air- and water-borne pollutants originating from agricultural and industrialized regions far to the south. Within the Arctic itself, there are local sources of pollution at abandoned mineral and hydrocarbon exploration and defence bases, town garbage dumps, and old mine sites. The presence of petroleum reserves offshore has been demonstrated and, given the right economic conditions, may one day be developed "in the national interest":

The biggest threat [to whaling] that I know, would be any accident in the off-shore drilling, in the water. That's the thing I am afraid of. There's no way, as far as I know, when there's a major blowout on the ice, that anybody on this Earth will be able to clean it up. There's no technology for it.

Edward Hopson, Sr., Barrow, April 1995

. . . I learned that offshore oil production is shortly to start. This is a great danger for all living things in the sea, and hence for us. . . . American geologists consoled us that in case of oil spills, oil companies will pay us [compensation]. But hunters do not eat paper bills, and animals will not become healthier thanks to these bills and the sea will not become purer. . . . They should not install offshore derricks under the very harsh ice conditions of our seas. Those that plan [these developments] live very far from here, and they don't care for our environment. . . . They are ready to destroy it for money.

Timofei Panaugye, Sireniki, February 1995

The reassurances offered to Inuit communities by industry and government—that such large-scale pollution events are unlikely to ever occur, and that cleaning up any spills will be undertaken with dispatch and good effect—are viewed with considerable scepticism by people living in the area:

. . . the industry and [federal Minerals Management Service] pretty much told us . . . there won't be a spill, and if there is—we can clean it up. We know that you CAN have spills, and as 99.9 percent of the people up here had suspected, you can't clean it up. . . . What are you going to do around here, where it's cold and dark, and you have to pay people a fantastic amount of money to go out in broken ice conditions and start waving a mop around? That's scary.

Tom Albert, Barrow, April 1995

Although it may appear reasonable to think of the Arctic as remaining relatively untouched, and indeed pure, because of its vast uninhabited expanses and its remoteness from heavily industrialized areas existing elsewhere, this is no longer a true picture. All the oceans of the world are connected, as is the atmosphere enveloping the Earth. Thus, pollutants entering any coastal waters in more temperate or industrialized regions will eventually reach the Arctic Ocean, while noxious gases leaving smokestacks anywhere in the world are eventually released as precipitation in Arctic regions. As an example of such long-range transport, radioactive contamination in the Arctic Ocean is dominated by wastes originating from nuclear facilities at Sellafield in the United Kingdom and Cap La Hague in France, and *not*, for example, from unsafe military installations in the Russian Arctic.

Sustainable Use, Indigenous Knowledge, and Conservation

Sustainable use is applicable only to renewable resources: it means using them at rates within their capacity for renewal.

World Conservation Strategy, 1980

The term "sustainability" or "sustainable use" is commonly used today with respect to resource use, but it is by no means widely accepted. Some point out that the term *sustainable* implies a continuation of use over a long period of time, but no one can say whether use levels that are sustainable over, say, the next half-dozen or so years will in fact be sustainable in twenty years' time. What if some unexpected environmental change occurs, and the resource population suddenly declines? Indeed, in such circumstances today's "sustainable" practices might be deemed (in hindsight!) to have been unsustainable.

This example suggests that management systems that are in place need to be capable of responding to such future events, so that corrective actions can be taken without undue delay. This requires ongoing monitoring of the resource stock, and for many managers and conservationists this is effectively accomplished during the act of using the resource. The term *adaptive management* is used to describe the management practice whereby the results of resource use are used to evaluate the health of the resource population on an ongoing basis. Such monitoring provides the managers with timely feedback on the consequences of ongoing management decisions. Thus, in the case of hunters or fishers, the actions of taking and processing food animals allows expert evaluations to be made on the physical condition of individual animals (and, in aggregate, the whole population). In such daily observing and cutting up of animals, any unexpected changes in behaviour or bodily condition can be assessed against a long-term standard of "normal" bodily and population health. It is for this reason that many Inuit insist that they are indeed the managers, the guardians of the animals—for they are usually the first to detect changes in the status of the resources.

This management capability of local resource users has indeed been recognized internationally. Thus, in 1987, the report of the World Commission on Environment and Development highlighted the importance of preserving the traditional knowledge and experience that exists within indigenous communities. The report observed that the loss of traditional knowledge and skills in sustainably managing complex ecosystems would be a loss to humankind. The Convention on Biological Diversity emphasizes the need to respect, preserve, and maintain the knowledge, innovations, and practices of indigenous communities that relate to the conservation and sustainable use of biodiversity.

These examples indicate that now the connection with social behaviour, and consequently well-being, is intimately related to the attainment of conservation objectives, where conservation (in the words of the 1980 World Conservation Strategy) is *"the management of human use of the biosphere so that it may yield the greatest sustainable benefit to the present generations while maintaining its potential to meet the needs and aspirations of future generations."* The Arctic Environmental Protection Strategy [AEPS] in a 1996 report commented:

... competing approaches to sustainable development share a number of common conclusions. They suggest that long-term social well-being, economic development, and environmental health are interdependent.

The problems Inuit confront in regard to such water- and air-borne pollutants entering their ecosystems are in some important respects different from the problems faced by those living outside of the Arctic. First, there are more biological "steps" in Arctic food chains than occur in agricultural food chains in the temperate or tropical zones, and at each step of the chain contaminants become progressively more concentrated. To illustrate this in a simplified manner, consider the steps taken to produce beef: a cow eats grass. In this case there are only three food-production steps: soil to grass, then grass to cow, and then cow to person. (This simple example ignores the fact that cattle often eat food concentrates that, in addition to containing grass products such as grain or hay, may contain fish or animal by-products.)

In contrast to this situation, in the Arctic there are many more biological steps in the production of marine-derived foods (which provide the staple diet of nearly all Inuit). The chemicals in the seawater are taken up by microscopic plants, then the microscopic plants are eaten by microscopic animals, which are eaten by small shrimp-like creatures, which in turn are eaten by fish (such as arctic cod or capelin), and then the fish are eaten by beluga or bowhead whale. This food chain may be longer, if, for example, small fish are eaten by larger fish, which likely happens in the case of beluga. Scientists estimate that at each stage of the food chain, pollutants may become about ten times more concentrated. Thus, in the case of eating beef, pollutants in the meat may occur at 100 times the concentration that occurs in the soil (that is, with only two steps in the chain, $10 \times 10 = 100$). However, in the case of the whale, the pollutant load is far heavier because there are several more links in the food chain, resulting in a contaminant's being about *100,000 times* more concentrated in whale meat than in seawater (that is, $10 \times 10 \times 10 \times 10 \times 10 = 100,000$).

There are two further reasons why marine foods pose a potential pollution problem to Inuit and other northern residents eating local foods. First, contaminants progressively accumulate during the lifetime of a plant or animal, so that the older the animal or plant becomes, the more contaminants will accumulate in its tissues. Arctic animals and plants tend to live longer than do related plants and animals in the temperate zone. Thus, whereas most beef cattle are slaughtered when less than two years old, a seal or whale may often be ten or twenty years old, or even older, when taken by a hunter.

Another problem faced by Inuit is that organochlorine pollutants (such as PCBs) concentrate in the fatty tissues of the body, and Inuit include more of the fat of the animals they eat than do people eating beef. With such dietary preferences, the Inuit diet has the potential to contain a greater amount of fat-soluble organochlorine contamination than would be the case if there were less fat in the diet. The same tendency for fat-soluble pollutants to concentrate in fatty tissues occurs in humans too. Inuit are aware, and many are worried, that nursing mothers pass on high concentrations of PCBs to their babies in their fat-rich milk; thus, the President of Pauktuutit, the Canadian Inuit Women's Association, speaking at a 1996 conference on contaminants and human health, observed: *"Once [Inuit] women reach adulthood, and are ready to have children, they already carry a lifetime's accumulation of PCBs that cannot be expelled from the body."* Tests carried out among nursing mothers in Nunavik (northern Quebec) indicated that their milk contained a number of pesticide and PCB-related residues at concentrations four to ten times greater than occurred in Caucasian nursing women living in southern Quebec. However, despite these relatively high contaminant loads in Inuit women, Dr. John P. Middaugh, a public health authority, writing about the comparable Alaskan situation noted *"no death, illness, cancer, birth defect, or other adverse toxicological effect has ever been found in an Alaskan caused by PCB, dioxin, DDT, DDE, mercury, cadmium, arsenic, ozone, arctic haze, radionuclides or radon."*

While this fortunate clinical outcome may be due to the health benefits derived from eating marine mammal–derived foods, nevertheless all these contaminants are invisible and odourless. As Inuit generally fear what they cannot see, the very notion that a whale may be contaminated causes alarm, and may dissuade some people from eating local foods when alternatives (even if less appetizing or nutritious) are available. Thus, the danger may not be from eating contaminated food, but in fact from avoiding local food.

In the 1960s, Inuit in Hudson Bay were advised to avoid whale mattak when it was found to contain elevated levels of mercury, and many complied with the advice. This advice was offered before health scientists understood that mattak contained selenium, a substance that effectively blocked mercury toxicity. However, more recently, many Inuit in Broughton Island (on Baffin Island) gave up eating whale and seal after being told that their food contained high concentrations of PCB. However, despite earlier concerns expressed by health professionals who were aware of the relatively high concentrations of various contaminants in the tissues of Arctic animals, the advice being offered to Inuit today considers a greater variety of factors than were taken into account in the past. Thu, Dr. Harriet Kuhnlein, Director of the Centre for Nutrition and the Environment of Indigenous Peoples, at McGill University, reflects today's more balanced understandings when writing:

The various benefits of fats (satiety, flavour, cultural values, fat-soluble vita-mins, unsaturated fats . . .) . . . should be balanced against advice to avoid traditional fats that contain particular contaminants. . . . In fact, it seems there are so many benefits for Indigenous People from using traditional Arctic food fats that their use should be promoted for a variety of cultural, eco-nomic, and nutritional reasons.

Indeed, the medical advice now appears to be that a diet based on fresh local foods presents far less risk to the health of Arctic residents than would result if imported foods were substituted. For not only are imported foods nutritionally inferior, they in turn carry an array of chemicals introduced through modern agricultural-production methods. Therefore, Inuit are coming to terms with the fact that their food inevitably contains some level of indus-trial contamination, however hard they try to avoid it. Although Inuit may, as a consequence of the global occurrence of a large variety of contaminants, be at little or no more risk than any other inhabitants of our polluted planet, the variety of differing opinions expressed by different commentators can itself cause confusion and alarm. It is also recognized that the situation requires care-ful monitoring because, in the case of long-term exposure to even low levels of contaminants, medical science is moving into relatively uncharted territory.

CULTURAL IMPERIALISM

. . . most of us have still a hunter culture as our basic identity and we cannot continue to be passive in the world while our lifestyles are exposed to emo-tional and foreign campaigns against our sustainable harvest of the wild ani-mals that nature gave us for life's sustainment.

Lars Emil Johansen, Premier of Greenland, speaking at a
United Nations meeting, New York, December 10, 1992

Perhaps the single greatest threat to the ongoing sustainable use of whales by Inuit is posed by aggressive attempts at cultural and ideological domination by groups of people wielding influence in the industrialized western world. The homogenization of ideas, cultures, knowledge, and realities taking place through global processes of urbanization and "westernization" represents a direct threat to the lifestyles, cultures, and well-being of many indigenous and rural peoples worldwide. This threat has been long recognized by Inuit:

FIGURE 28. Narwhal mattak eaten fresh and raw. Melville Bay, North Greenland, 1988.

The people living in big cities . . . are in conflict with the aboriginal peoples. . . . It is easier for the environmentalists to attack the hunting peoples instead of doing something about the pollution the heavy industries are creating. They are not at all aware what danger they are causing for the cultural survival of the Inuit in the Arctic areas, and what great threat they cause to many species, humankind included.

"Whaling in Greenland," KNAPK, June 1987

Thus, Inuit recognize that the most immediate threat to their whaling comes from the animal-protection movement and its successful co-opting of the media, public attitudes, and some government agencies. It is no mystery that campaigns to "Save the Whale," "Save the Seal," and various other animal protection causes originated in the urban centres of the industrialized world. In such centres, where nature has been pushed aside and then reintroduced in repackaged ways that cause no offence to urbanites' sensibilities, and where the realities of making a living in remote rural communities are beyond most people's comprehension, campaigns against the killing of noble and defenceless animals have succeeded to a remarkable degree.

Far removed from the life-through-death reality of feeding one's family that remains the everyday circumstance for half of humankind, urban people have become further removed from this basic understanding by the emotionalism of artfully presented animal-protection campaigns. As a consequence, something that pretends to be a conservation movement now glorifies and espouses the nonconsumptive use of whales and many other elements of the natural world. These campaigns find favour with many people wishing to support what they believe to be environmental causes and having the additional attraction of working to end the suffering of innocent animals. Indeed, the "Save the Whale" movement, in particular, has captured the public's imagination like no other "environmental" campaign. The awe-inspiring body size of whales, and their presumed rarity, song, "intelligence," and other appealing qualities, make their continued use by Inuit and other coastal peoples an emotionally charged and highly problematic issue for many non-Native people. While television and newspaper pictures of whales being killed shock and offend people who, in their everyday lives, avoid thinking about death, such pictures serve as a vivid reminder of humankind's questionable treatment of other life forms. Saving whales has become a focus and powerful symbol of what can and must be done to reverse these tendencies. Greenland writer Finn Lynge has described western industrialized people's worrisome relationship with nonhuman nature in these terms:

> . . . the human being[s] on top of creation, with the legally unchallenged right to destroy animal habitats, wage unnecessarily cruel wars against pest animals, toxify the food chain, and enslave so-called domestic animals by the millions, if not billions, for industrial execution. . . . The fact remains that animals do have problems with humans—bad problems.

For those who abhor humankind's questionable relationship with animalkind, a new ideology, one that advances the belief that animals have rights at least equal to those of humans, offers people a way to feel better about themselves. The means to this desirable end is, in concert with other concerned citizens, to join a movement that promises to work tirelessly to end these offending practices. Very little is asked of the citizen—merely a periodic contribution of money, no more than the cost of a book, or of a restaurant meal.

It is doubtful if many of those who contribute to such appeals realize the extent of damage these animal-protection campaigns cause the very people who care most about marine mammals and who have the greatest stake in these animals' continuing health and survival. The best-known cases of this damage occurred as a result of antisealing campaigns of the 1970s and 1980s, campaigns based on the twin falsehoods that harp seals were endangered and that the method of killing them was unspeakably cruel and inhumane. In a few short years after the consequent collapse of the seal-skin market in 1983, a variety of social pathologies—which included very high rates of suicide, as well as escalating social assistance payments and loss of self-respect—increased alarmingly in Arctic Canada and Greenland. The President of the Inuit Circumpolar Conference (ICC), speaking at a Nordic Council of Ministers conference on trade, observed:

> Sale of sealskins was once the main source of cash income for many Inuit families. The loss of this source of revenue has been catastrophic. But the consequences go far beyond the economic. Seal hunting has always been an extremely important part of our traditional culture and values. A recent ICC study of the Arctic Sealing Industry confirms that the collapse of this market has had severe and negative social, cultural, nutritional, and psychological effects on many Inuit.
>
> *Rosemarie Kuptana, speaking in Copenhagen, January 1996*

FIGURE 29. Hunters preparing narwhal mattak for sale. Qaanaaq, Greenland, August 1988.

However, animal welfare organizations care little that their activities can, and often do, have devastating social, cultural, economic, and health impacts on traditional users of marine mammals and other living resources. There is a huge financial incentive to continue such campaigns, and indeed the campaigns' very success encourages their organizers to believe that there exists a public need for such activities. However, the appearance of need exists largely because the public lacks relevant and factual information on the issues being targeted.

Unfortunately, the poorly informed public also includes politicians who, in turn, often embrace emotive animal-welfare causes as a way of being seen to support popular "environmental" or "green" causes. The German parliament passed a resolution, in November 1996, that calls on the IWC to restrict all sale of whale meat and mattak taken by Inuit hunters; the resolution requires that all whale products remain with the whalers and be used for their own consumption. Thus, the well-functioning and two-centuries-old Greenland monetized trading and food-distribution system is to be disrupted by people who probably have never visited, nor indeed know anything useful about, Greenland. It is doubtful that those voting for such a resolution know how the consequences of their vote (if successful) will adversely impact the health and well-being of Greenlanders. Do German parliamentarians think that Greenland hunters (as food producers) differ from German farmers (as food producers), and consequently do not need to pay for the equipment they use to produce food? *"Obviously, whalers running whaling operations from their own fishing boats must also be given the chance to cover their costs and be paid for their work . . . [T]oday's Greenland cannot function without a money economy,"* commented Hansi Kreutzmann, of the Greenland Hunters and Fishermen's Association. Such a restriction would also impact the Chukotkan whalers particularly severely, and the justification for such action would be quite incomprehensible:

> I don't know why we can't sell some of our whale production, [for] we have only the one source of income—marine mammals—and we need not only food but other things. You brought us into the market economy, and [now] you are not permitting us to sell anything. This is surprising!
>
> *Timofei Panangye, Sireniki, February 1995*

> It would be good if part of our production could be sold—hunters don't have cash at all . . . and we can't buy many of the things we need for lack of money. When you are visiting someone you need cash to pay for your fare; you won't buy a ticket with blubber and meat.
>
> *Petr Typkhkak, Sireniki, February 1996*

Despite an indifference, if not an outright wish, to impoverish hunters living under quite difficult conditions, the "Save the Whale," "Save the Seal," and other similar animal-rights campaigns are successful enough to maintain the directors of the sponsoring organizations in well-paying jobs in multi-million-dollar corporations. These corporations accumulate vast sums of money that are then used to influence politicians' views and actions. For example, the Humane Society of the United States (which actively opposes whaling) reported spending over $20 million on its campaigns in 1994, while having cash and securities of over $46 million on hand. Two other "smaller" U.S. anti-whaling groups, the Friends of Animals and the Fund for Animals, had annual budgets of about $4 million and $5 million, respectively.

Commenting on the situation during the early years of the "Save the Seal" campaign, Finn Lynge writes:

> . . . Inuit income fell to an all-time low of about $100 [per hunter]. However, the anti-seal hunt organizations were strengthened financially to a remarkable degree. In the middle of the 1980s, IFAW [International Fund for Animal Welfare] made more than $6 million on its seal hunt campaign. In the United States alone, the seal pups reaped $5 million for Greenpeace. Defenders of Wildlife (USA) got over $1.7 million in 1981 and the Center for Environmental Education (also USA) which specialized in the anti–seal hunt campaign, made $2.2 million in 1980. . . . Greenpeace operates with ships . . . and helicopters. . . . In 1982 IFAW used $1 million in half a year just for newsletters and postage...[and] a million dollars for a house with offices and computer equipment, as well as a . . . helicopter and an airplane. In 1984 IFAW threatened to get involved in a Canadian parliamentary election by means of a $3 million political campaign aimed at candidates that supported the seal hunt.

Such levels of support for political purposes continue. The IFAW, through an affiliate organization headed by five IFAW staff members, gave about $2 million to the British Labour party for the 1997 election campaign. Considering the large-scale financial and human resources these animal-protection organizations can apply to their political causes, the ability of Inuit to counter the damage caused by this industry is obviously quite limited. In comparison with animal-protection organizations, which are large in size and number, and both economically and politically advantaged (in the latter case, by maintaining lobbyists in various national capitals), Inuit communities and organizations are small in size, few in number, economically weak, and politically marginal. The understanding and support of rational people is urgently required if Inuit are to rebuild their damaged economies using the resources available to them:

We need the protection of the international community against the campaigns which are launched towards our wildlife products on purely ethnocentric grounds: products which are harvested in full accordance with the international standards for sustainable use. In general, we need the help and support of the world community in order to develop and protect our own economic opportunities on the world market.

Lars Emil Johansen, Premier of Greenland, to UN Working Group
on Indigenous Populations, New York, July 1993

THE CONTINUING APPEAL OF THE GLORY DAYS OF ENVIRONMENTAL ACTIVISM

Environmentalists are the biggest problem. We have to bring people to understand how we hunt the whale . . . during our whaling captains' meeting, there was a letter from one . . . group—they wanted to get on a whaling ship! They don't understand: we hunt from open boats, umiaqs. The environmentalists are there at the IWC. . . . They are against whaling, no matter whose culture they hurt.

Jeslie Kaleak, Sr., Barrow, April 1995

In the 1970s, growing international awareness of the deteriorating state of the environment resulted in a number of determined efforts to improve the global situation. The growth and proliferation of citizen-supported environmental organizations in many western industrial countries was phenomenal and quickly attracted media attention, causing governments and intergovernmental organizations to take note of this widespread public concern.

The current concern with *sustainable development,* today an acknowledged partner of responsible environmentalism, was almost unheard of during the 1970s. The concern then was almost exclusively directed toward *environmental protection.* In those days, it seemed that almost everything in the environment was in urgent need of protection: every river, shoreline, ocean, Antarctica, indeed every species of animal and plant—and, for some, every individual animal and plant. Perhaps this last was a case of overreaction, but the environmental movement and its message were earnestly embraced by many idealistic young people who were, understandably, worried about their future on a planet that, in their view, was being assaulted grievously from all sides. The risks appeared daunting: nuclear threat, overconsumption (and attendant massive overproduction of wastes), and an unending and self-centred preoccupation

FIGURE 30. Hunters waiting for bowhead at the floe edge. Barrow, Alaska, May 1992.

with ever more industrial growth and consequent resource depletion, all seemingly without concern for the consequences of such behaviour. Who could be blamed if some exaggeration or emotion were added to campaign rhetoric, in an attempt to get someone in authority to listen?

It was by shocking exaggeration that the movements in the 1970s increased first the size of their memberships and then their financial and political influence. At first there appeared various generalist organizations, such as Greenpeace or Friends of the Earth, that could publicize many environmental issues and thereby sensitize and appeal to a wide range of concerned people. Other organizations, like the World Wildlife Fund (WWF), focused more on those animal species that people would easily recognize and be concerned about: pandas, tigers, whales, elephants. At that time, when "the environment" was many people's priority for charitable giving, there was room enough for many specialist groups: thus, Project Jonah, the Whale and Dolphin Conservation Society, and the Connecticut Cetacean Society, which focused people's concerns on the whales (and to a lesser extent, dolphins) of the world, which they claimed were on the verge of extinction. However, in the case of these more narrowly focused groups, their appeal was that they were not just concerned with saving species from becoming extinct; rather, they also had the goal of saving *individual* whales or dolphins that were in danger of being killed, whether or not that death affected the biological status of the population or species as a whole. Thus an individual sperm whale (out of more than some one million sperm whales worldwide) was thought equally deserving of being "saved," as was an individual blue whale or northern right whale (where perhaps only a thousand or fewer animals of these particular species were thought to exist). The whales were (and continue to be) individualized and named, and offered for adoption—in the same manner as are the desperate and appealing children in less-developed parts of the world.

This belief in the sanctity of every individual whale's life still exists today. Thus, whale-saving organizations continue to work to protect every individual whale or dolphin without regard to the extent of its rarity or abundance. It is this concern for the individual animal's welfare that continues to confront and oppose Inuit (and others') hunting of whales for food, even when the species in question are nonendangered and their hunted populations may be growing in size. However, such opposition to whaling today is not generally justified by "scientific" arguments, as was the situation in earlier times. Instead, the justification for holding and advancing protectionist views today is largely subjective, or cultural, and continues to be supported by people who find that scientific arguments do little to dispel the discomfort experienced by the thought that large, wild, warm-blooded animals are being killed and eaten.

Such sentiments, as mentioned earlier, are most prevalent among urban, middle-class people in industrialized countries. Those directing these animal-protection campaigns demonstrate a decidedly ethnocentric and limiting view of the world, together with a total disregard, if not disdain, for people whose culture, lifestyle, and occupational choices are different from their own. These large animal-welfare organizations represent a political force whose potency remains, despite competing ideas selectively embraced by most governments that advocate the sustainable use of resources. One reason for this continuing potency of "animal welfarism" is that the politicians appealed to usually share the protesters' own limited understanding of, and apparent disregard for, human societies different from their own.

State and international resource management regimes often reflect the values and attitudes of the people they represent, which again necessarily places the user community in a decidedly minority position. In such cases, considering the resources available to the protest industry to influence decision-making, the antiwhaling movement has had a profound influence on the policies and activities of urban-based bureaucracies. Thus, when national governments and international organizations become involved in Inuit whaling, even the creation of successful comanagement regimes may not completely end future challenges to the sustainable use of whales by Inuit.

THE IMPOSITION OF STATE MANAGEMENT CONCEPTS

> The concept of wildlife is taken from a farming culture. . . . We do not use the concept of wildlife. My reason for questioning these concepts is that the policy makers, the biologists and administrators outside our world are foreign to hunting and the hunting cultures. . . . So ban the concepts of "managing" "stocks," the concepts like "harvesting," the concepts of "wildlife" [and] through the process of changing your vocabulary, you may be understood better by the people you serve . . . or [who] hired you to create a sustainable culture for themselves and the generations to come.
>
> *Ingmar Egede, Nuuk, speaking at an international*
> *conference in Inuvik, November 20, 1995*

Yet another form of cultural imperialism that sometimes serves to undermine the sustainable use of whales by Inuit may result from the imposition on local communities of state management procedures, concepts, and knowledge. For generations, Inuit have relied on their own systems of local management and the knowledge that informs such systems, in order to survive and to reproduce the material, institutional, and cultural foundations of their societies. However, the imposition of a state management system on these local-level arrangements may adversely affect the long-standing relationship the user community has developed with the living resources on which it depends, a relationship that continually reinforces that society's fundamental connection to the land and its living resources.

Some Inuit, as described earlier, have negotiated comanagement arrangements with their respective national governments as a means of seeking to limit this form of cultural domination; in some cases, these comanagement bodies are working well. However, in other situations, comanagement—regardless of how many Inuit sit on such boards—is perceived by the hunters most directly affected as little more than imposing on local Inuit lifestyles and values the state-management model and the scientific traditions that underpin it. Rosemarie Kuptana, past President of the Inuit Circumpolar Conference, recently stated:

> With various culturally inappropriate or irrelevant concepts such as "wildlife management," terminology such as "stock" (and) "harvest," and procedures such as "total allowable catches" (and) "quotas," the state management system is a form of intrusion that threatens to crush the "tried and true," the dynamic, evolving, and effective systems of local management and the local knowledge that informs those systems.

Comanagement in Inuit regions is sometimes legitimated by seeking out Inuit traditional ecological knowledge (TEK) with a view to informing management decisions and programmes. However, many Inuit feel strongly about this issue, and are reluctant to share their local knowledge with outside interests, for good reasons. Rosemarie Kuptana continued:

> Our traditional ecological knowledge is too often taken out of context, misinterpreted, or misused. What wildlife managers, biologists, and bureaucrats understand, or think they see, is interpreted within their own knowledge and value systems, not ours. In the process, our special ways of knowing and doing things (for example, our local systems of management) are crushed by scientific knowledge and the state management model. What many Qallunaat [non-Inuit] fail to appreciate is that our traditional ecological knowledge exists in a larger context or frame of reference that is very different from theirs. Inuit also possess knowledge that is not traditional, and that is not con-

nected to the environment. It is important to recognize that all aspects of our knowledge forms a unique system of knowledge that we use to interpret the world around [us], as it has been for thousands of years, and as it changes.

The quest for Inuit TEK by comanagement regimes may serve to polarize and then generate conflict between those who possess this knowledge and want to control how it is collected, interpreted, and used (for example, Inuit at the local level) and those who want or need this knowledge to fulfill their mandates (such as comanagement boards). This is especially the case if local Inuit believe that they are not deriving any real benefit from sharing their knowledge; ICC past President Kuptana again:

True comanagement should not use our traditional ecological knowledge for its own validation. Indigenous peoples are not content to "co-operate" while wildlife managers, biologists, and bureaucrats "manage." True comanagement can only exist when our proven systems of local knowledge and management, in their entirety, are considered equally with scientific knowledge and in resource decision-making. Then, and only then, will we be true partners in comanagement.

THE LONGING FOR A RETURN TO EDEN

Those involved in resource management (when nonmembers of the user community) may take a somewhat theoretical or idealized position (derived from their academic training) toward a given issue; this is not entirely unexpected, as it is their formal academic training that provides such managers with the credentials required for their job. If doubts exist as to the appropriate management course to recommend, certainly it is much more prudent to advance a conservative rather than a progressive—and less well-known—view that might be challenged vigorously by a majority of one's colleagues and political masters. Thus, the politically correct policy is one that aims to restore whale numbers to their "pre-exploitation levels."

However, the goal of restoring depleted whale populations to their supposed pre-exploitation levels is a scientifically unsound notion; it may also be impossible to achieve. The notion that there existed a particular pre-exploitation population level that could, or should, be reattained and then maintained is a commonly stated marine-mammal management goal, though it is an ecological absurdity. For not only is it impossible to know or validate, with any degree of confidence, the size of whale populations that frequented particular localities in the past, but such a notion assumes an ecological stability that has never existed. It suggests that there once existed a knowable, pristine, stable ocean community—an unchanging salt-water Eden. Ecological science, in contrast, points to dynamic and highly complex communities of animals and plants in competitive interaction, in which species vary in abundance as climates, say, and more local conditions—such as ice-cover, temperature, salinity, nutrient availability, biological productivity—allow some species to gain a consequent competitive advantage over others. Under such dynamic circumstances, no knowable equilibrium population, no stable "baseline," no "normal" population level, existed for any population of whale, seal, seabird, fish, or plankton species. The ocean remains a dynamic and complex environment where systemic changes within complex interdependent animal and plant communities are continually taking place.

Even if it were possible to know the unknowable, and to calculate an imaginary "pristine" population of beluga or bowhead whales, subsequent changes to that earlier ecosystem have so altered prior conditions (or "carrying capacity") as to render a return to these earlier population levels of questionable purpose or value as a conservation goal. Given that several species of whales, seals, fish, and seabirds may eat the same food organisms, who is to decide that it is better to reduce the biodiversity, or the integrity of a complex functioning ecosystem, in order to add a few hundred individuals to some particular species' population, at the expense of some other species' population numbers? In terms of animals' food requirements, adding a single whale to the ocean may well remove the food needed to sustain many thousands, or tens of thousands, of seabirds, or hundreds of thousands or more of food fish.

Given these imponderable questions, what might be considered a more realistic, prudent, and indeed moral objective is to manage and conserve sustainable human–whale relationships far into the future for the mutual benefit of both. However, a persistent problem for Inuit (and also for many other rural societies that need to consumptively use living resources) is the apparent difficulty that many urban peoples have in understanding ecological relationships that necessarily include people as part of nature. For too long, environmentalists have represented people as a cancer on the face of the Earth: too many people, growing at too fast a rate, threatening to destroy the host "organism" on which future existence depends.

The anti-whaling and animal-rights movement share this decidedly negative view of the place of humans in nature. It is an ideology that best flourishes among people living far removed from natural environments, or living far from people who depend on the environment for their livelihood. In the words of one environmental scientist and lawyer, Nancy Doubleday:

> [This] is an unnatural philosophy that assists in destroying nature rather than saving it, simply because it weakens the connection between human beings and their ecosystems, driving more people into direct dependency upon the industrial economy which represents a greater threat to the environment than regulated local-level use of renewable resources.

Many aboriginal people are acutely aware of the seriousness of the "disconnect" referred to above. An aboriginal perspective on this problem was provided by a Canadian First Nation speaker at an international environmental conference, commenting on the manner in which nonaboriginal speakers introduced themselves to fellow conference participants:

> Every introduction was about yourself, not about your community. You seem to have no community connections. In our culture, we identify ourselves in relation to our group. We don't know who we are except in relation to our family, our community, and the land that is our life. . . . Our first law is the law of the natural world that gave us life. . . . You can't imagine the pain your society creates by breaking up our connections to our land and our community. . . . Your disconnections with *your* community ruins ours.
>
> *Jeanette Armstrong, speaking at the Esalen Institute, California, 1993*

THE PRECAUTIONARY APPROACH: STALLING WITH PRINCIPLE

> Many conventional environmentalists advocate the "precautionary principle," which says that humanity must not interfere with nature until all the consequences of an action can be taken into account. But it is impossible to know all the consequences of even the most trivial action. . . . The new smarter environmentalism must also understand that there is no perfect solution to any problem; tradeoffs have to be made. The good cannot be held hostage to the perfect.
>
> *Ronald Bailey, in* The True State of the Planet, *1995*

A shortage or absence of scientific information is frequently considered sufficient reason for deciding that hunting should be stopped until scientists can provide the "right" decision. However, such lack of scientific knowledge may be an insufficient reason for suspending user groups' access to a renewable resource. This may especially be the case when and where Inuit and other indigenous peoples, depending on the continuing use of natural resources to meet their nutritional, social, economic, and cultural needs, state their belief that the local populations remain at healthy levels. Erring on the side of extreme caution may appear to constitute a justifiable action to nonresource users (such as the conservation bureaucracy, animal protectionists, and urban dwellers, among others), but when considered from a user-community perspective, such caution may appear to be decidedly less justified. Local resource users have been making decisions about using living resources for generations in the total absence of biologists and scientifically validated sources of information; it seems reasonable to believe, therefore, that the users possess experience-based and relevant information on the question of prudent resource use.

In many cases, nonusers' perceptions that the resource requires protection may merely be an artifact, the result of an absence of scientific information about how many animals are likely to exist in the population. In such circumstances, it might be reasonable to consider that others closer to the resource may possess additional information on the status of the resource. However, local resource users are all too aware that their own knowledge is often considered unreliable or otherwise unacceptable, particularly if it contradicts the conclusions already reached by the nonlocal managers or "experts." When such disputed population estimations by nonlocal managers are used to justify restrictions on continued use, it should be remembered that local community members may possess considerably more relevant information on the animal population, informed not only by their physical proximity to and familiarity with local resource species at the present time, but also by knowledge of past behaviour of the population over an extended period of time. Fluctuations in local resource abundance are nothing new to people having generation on generation of accumulated knowledge about the inherent variability of Arctic animal populations. Statements such as the following are commonplace when local people speak of the resources they see and depend on for their livelihood:

> There is no sign that the number of blue whales is increasing in our coastal areas, but I have noticed that the numbers of humpback whales, fin whales, and sperm whales have been increasing. [In the 1940s] . . . there were a lot of humpback whales that migrated into the fiords in fall. In the 1960s the number was decreasing, but now there [are signs] that the number is increasing again. In the last years, the number of humpback whales has increased remarkably. They are very common in summertime and stay in our waters

even into the fall. The same is true of fin whales. There is no sign the minke whales are decreasing in number.

Morten Heinrich, Greenland, June 1987

In fact, the precautionary principle, imposed from distant decision-making centres and advocating nonuse and the consequent potential to seriously disrupt human–animal codependency, may be an exceedingly unsound conservation strategy in the Inuit context, or when ecosystems are understood to include humans too.

Although sound management cannot be carried out in the absence of information, some management bodies behave today as though this was not only possible and reasonable, but also desirable. Thus, some member countries of the IWC that actively oppose whaling also oppose whale research that, in the opinion of whale biologists, will lead to better understanding of whale ecology, reproduction, and population dynamics. Those holding such views commonly operate with the ecologically unsound belief that, if whaling were stopped, then the cetacean component of the ocean biological community would, in time, return to its pre-exploitation (and presumed optimum) size and composition. It is quite likely that, in time, some degree of population increase will occur for most depleted whale populations. However, as explained earlier, there is no particular ideal or optimal population level that must be reached in the shortest time in order either to "save" the ecosystem or to re-create some ideal or "proper" marine balance.

An even more serious failing of the precautionary principle is the construction of, and then belief in, false opposites: that policy options involve deciding between risk or no-risk, of choosing between destruction (or security) of animal populations based simply on the presence (or absence) of hunting. In reality, the precautionary principle does not ensure the elimination of risk or damage to a population, for substituting one particular management action for another merely results in the replacement of one set of risks or damage by another set. An example of this is provided by the harp seal situation in the northwest Atlantic. Here, the ban on the killing of seal pups—a thoroughly sound conservation strategy, as it leaves the reproductively active adults free to continue breeding—has resulted in an unprecedented increase in the size of the population, which, according to Inuit and biologists' knowledge, is beginning to threaten biodiversity in many areas of the eastern Canadian and West Greenland Arctic and subarctic. Indeed, in some areas of western Greenland today, harp seals occur in such large numbers as to be unwelcome visitors—now referred to by some disparagingly as the "rats of the sea"—because their presence in such numbers keeps whales out of the bays and fiords, thereby reducing the local availability of food and forage-fish species.

Opponents of whaling sometimes claim that the precautionary principle justifies a blanket ban on whaling. One concern expressed by people opposed to whaling is that whaling, if allowed or encouraged, would result in a return to earlier practices when uncontrolled overexploitation drove whale populations down to unacceptably low levels. However, such an outcome is highly unrealistic (one might reasonably suggest it is quite impossible) when the differences between past and present circumstances are compared. The recent past history of commercial whaling illustrates the extent of this improbability. For example, in the late 1960s and early 1970s, because of the failure of the then-IWC to control the overhunting of large whales, the consequent uncertainty about the future security of the supply of whale oil caused industry to search for cheap and reliable substitutes. Shortly thereafter, petroleum-based machine oils and "hardened" vegetable oils were developed, and very quickly replaced the need for whale oil on the global market. By the 1980s, the ready availability of these cheap and abundant substitutes (consequently ending the global demand for whale oil) caused most major whaling nations to cease whaling. Those few that continued, though on a progressively reduced scale, whaled principally to provide meat to the few societies where whale meat has historically been included in the diet.

In complete contrast to this earlier situation, in today's world the absence of any global demand for whale products, the lack of profitability attendant on the imposition of exceedingly conservative quotas by the IWC, and trade restrictions banning the importation of whale products into most of the major former whale-consuming countries, all conspire to make economically impossible any return to the large-scale whaling operations of the past. Although the present limited supply may initially cause prices to rise, at a certain point in time the high price will very likely begin to reduce market demand for the product. Consequently, given the balance of market forces, whalers truly have limited incentive to seek to flood the market with meat, as prices paid for the meat would quickly drop.

A DOMINO EFFECT

It is difficult for outsiders to comprehend the intimacy of these [interactions between the hunter and the environment] because their relationship to the natural world is so different. The Eskimos' language, folklore, world view, ethics, education, and epistemology have all grown from the land, sea, atmosphere, and animals that surround them. Thus, Eskimo culture is a manifestation in human terms of the environment that has been its sustaining foundation.

IWC Panel Meeting of Experts on Aboriginal/Subsistence Whaling, Seattle, February 1979

Cultural imperialism, as a direct threat to the sustainable use of living resources by Inuit and other indigenous peoples, has many faces. The antiwhaling, anti-sealing, and anti-trapping movements are among the most obvious. But there are others—less overt, but no less damaging. Recent international efforts establishing whale sanctuaries covering the Indian Ocean and, linking with it, the southern oceans surrounding the Antarctic, are now being followed by calls for an Arctic whale sanctuary. Setting aside such extensive areas, where the killing of abundant, nonendangered marine mammals would be prohibited in the name of conservation, would create initiatives whose justification or purpose will be difficult for most Inuit (and many non-Inuit conservationists) to comprehend. Such questionable initiatives are deeply troubling, as there appears to be no legal recourse to stem such imperialistic ambitions:

The northern hemisphere is next. That's my biggest fear right now. . . . I know eventually the IWC will come up with the sanctuary in the northern hemisphere. . . .

Inupiaq, Barrow, April 1995

Inuit are very much aware of the history of European and Yankee whaling, a form of whaling that they understand depleted whale populations to a serious extent. Roger Silook, a St. Lawrence Island whaler, wrote in 1981: "*We whalers must pay for the greed of the 19th century commercial whalers who hunted bowhead whales to near extinction . . . [M]ust we . . . endure hunger and starvation just as we did when . . . Westerners first passed through our homeland?*" However, this morally questionable form of resource use, motivated by a desire to accumulate more and more wealth by wasteful means, is a form of whaling that Inuit neither condone nor practice. That such excesses of the past, committed by others, now lead to international restrictions against their own modest needs is widely recognized and resented, especially by young Inuit:

> If the colonists [commercial whalers] didn't hunt whales in the 1800s and early 1900s, there would be many whales still around. Why punish the Inuit for something that the colonists did?
>
> *Phill Robinson, Attaguttaaluk School, Igloolik, February 1995*

> It is not the Inuit who almost killed them all, and therefore it is not right for anyone to take away the freedom and rights of the Inuit. . . . All the sea mammals are here to help us humans.
>
> *Angela Gibbons, Sakku School, Coral Harbour, March 1995*

> The Inuit never killed the bowhead whale by the thousands; the species was never in any danger while in Inuit hands. . . . The commercial whalers harvested them by the thousands . . . [consequently] there has been a generation that has lost a part of their culture. That generation is my generation. I do not understand the loss of the bowhead. Why? There is one reason and one reason only: my culture, or at least a part of it, was stolen from me."
>
> *Adina Duffy, Sakku School, Coral Harbour, March 1995*

Those who have been cultured in the scientific tradition might entertain the thought that there are many different realities. Diverse cultures have diverse ways of experiencing, understanding, and interpreting reality and, in sum, defining it. To suggest, as many appear to, that there is only one reality—the universal truth of scientific knowledge or the particular rationality of western industrialized society—perpetuates a colonial mindset and fosters a form of cultural imperialism that is both objectionable and exceedingly unhelpful in the search for international solutions to important global questions. Reality is always culturally scripted. The foundations of cross-cultural cooperation would be significantly strengthened if those enculturated in the scientific, or Euro-American, or techno-industrial, tradition could accept as true the notion that they are as much a product of their own culture as Inuit are of theirs, and that no single cultural tradition has a monopoly on "the truth."

Such overbearing attitudes and consequent actions by metropolitan animal-protection interests, in different ways and in regard to different adaptations, undermine the rights and capacity (though not the will) of Inuit to use whales and other living resources in a sustainable and socially enriching manner. Yet to the extent that such actions that attack Inuit cultural practices and traditions succeed, they contribute to a dangerous "domino effect" that progressively weakens the centuries-old adaptive relationship Inuit have established with the living resources on which they continue to depend. This undermining of a remarkably long-lived ecological relationship, in one of the most demanding environments on the face of the Earth, can only result in a serious loss—for all of humankind—of environmental understanding, sensitivity, and, as a consequence, adaptive fitness. Any such loss is increasingly understood as constituting a threat to the industrialized world, which may have much to learn from Inuit and other indigenous peoples about the sustainable use of living resources—a sustainable use that, in the final analysis, provides the key to our collective survival on this planet.

SUGGESTED READINGS

Arctic Environmental Protection Strategy [AEPS]. 1996. *Report of the Task Force on Sustainable Development and Utilization, and Working Papers in Progress*. Ottawa.

Bailey, R. (ed.). 1995. *The True State of the Planet*. New York: The Free Press.

Canadian Polar Commission. 1996. *For Generations to Come: Contaminants, the Environment, and Human Health in the Arctic*. Polaris Papers No. 10, Ottawa.

Dewailly, E., et al. 1992. Breast milk contamination by PCDDs, PCDFs, and PCBs in Arctic Quebec: A preliminary assessment. *Chemosphere* 25:1245–49.

Donovan, G. P. (ed.). 1982. Report of the Cultural Anthropology Panel, pp. 35–49 in *Aboriginal/Subsistence Whaling (with special reference to the Alaska and Greenland fisheries)*. Reports of the International Whaling Commission Special Issue 4, Cambridge, England.

Doubleday, N. 1994. Arctic whales: Sustaining indigenous peoples and conserving arctic resources. In: M. M. R. Freeman and U. P. Kreuter (eds.), *Elephants and Whales: Resources for Whom?* pp. 239–59. Basel: Gordon and Breach.

Freeman, M. M. R. 1991. Energy, food security and A.D. 2040: The case for sustainable utilization of whale stocks. *Resource Management and Optimization* 8(3–4):235–44.

———. 1994. Science and trans-science in the whaling debate. In: M. M. R. Freeman and U. P. Kreuter (eds.), *Elephants and Whales: Resources for Whom?* pp. 143–57. Basel: Gordon and Breach.

Hodge, R. A. (ed.). 1995. *Pathways to Sustainability: Assessing our Progress*. Ottawa: National Round Table on Environment and Economy.

Inuit Circumpolar Conference (ICC). 1995. *Circumpolar Whaling and the ICC Whaling Agenda: A Choice for Inuit to Make.* (Available from Inuit Circumpolar Conference, 170 Laurier Ave. W., Suite 504, Ottawa, Ontario, Canada, K1P 5V5.)

Kershaw, P., and A. Baxter. 1995. The transfer of reprocessing wastes from northwest Europe to the Arctic. *Deep Sea Research II* 42:1413–48.

Kuhnlein, H. V. 1994. Dietary fat in traditional and contemporary indigenous food systems. *Arctic Medical Research* 53, Supplement 2:285–88.

Kuptana, R. 1996. *Indigenous Peoples' Right to Self-determination and Development: Issues of Equality and Decolonisation.* Keynote Address, International Seminar on Development and Self-Determination Among the Indigenous Peoples of the North. University of Alaska, Fairbanks. Oct. 5, 1996. (Available from Inuit Circumpolar Conference, 170 Laurier Avenue W., Suite 504, Ottawa, Ontario, Canada, K1P 5V5.)

Lynge, F. 1992. *Arctic Wars: Animal Rights, Endangered Peoples.* Hanover, NH, and London: University Press of New England.

Middaugh, J. P. 1994. Implications for human health of arctic environmental contamination. *Arctic Research of the United States* 8:214–19.

Nordic Council of Ministers. 1996. *Indigenous Peoples Production and Trade.* TemaNord 1996:553, Copenhagen.

Pfirman, S., R. Schlosser, and R. Macdonald. 1996. Assessment of contaminant risk in the Arctic. *Arctic Research in the United States* 10:11–23.

Sanderson, K., and G. W. Gabrielsen (eds.). 1996. Marine Mammals and the Marine Environment. *The Science of the Total Environment* 186 (1–2).

Usher, P. J., M. Baikie, M. Demmer, D. Nakashima, M. G. Stevenson, and M. Stiles. 1995. *Communicating About Contaminants in Country Food: The Experience in Aboriginal Communities.* (Available from Inuit Tapirisat of Canada, 170 Laurier Avenue W., Suite 510, Ottawa, Ontario, Canada, K1P 5V5.)

CHAPTER SIX

Securing the Future of Inuit Whaling

THE ICC WHALING AGENDA

Experience has led us to understand that indigenous people must take part in the management of whales and other animal resources, as is the case in Alaska, Canada, and Greenland. . . . We have all understood that we shall only be able to get something from our authorities by creating a union of marine hunters of Chukotka and by then uniting with respective organizations of Alaska, Canada, and Greenland.

Lyudmila Ainana, Provideniya, 1995

At the 1992 Inuit Circumpolar Conference (ICC) General Assembly, delegates discussed issues threatening Inuit rights to continue hunting whales. This discussion was prompted by increasing disregard for these rights by many animal-protection organizations and several governments during meetings of the International Whaling Commission. Thus, the ICC General Assembly passed resolution 92-17, which requested the ICC Executive Council to explore various options that might make more secure the Inuit–whale relationship in the face of these persistent and disruptive attacks on whaling societies.

This ICC resolution was strongly supported by delegates from each of the four Inuit homelands at the 1992 General Assembly. The vision at the time appeared to strongly favour a pan-Inuit whaling commission that would assume some degree of management responsibility over those whale (and small cetacean) species hunted by Inuit. However, the financial resources required to establish such an organization were recognized as being large; in addition,

Inuit in some countries were making progress in improving their relationship with their own national governments through the implementation of cooperative management agreements or by other means.

Therefore, quite apart from the financial difficulties to be overcome, attempts to accommodate these diverse within-country arrangements in a single international management regime promised to be extremely difficult. For example, though the Canada–Greenland Joint Commission on Narwhal and Beluga appears to be continuing to work in a fully cooperative manner, the failure of the Alaska–Inuvialuit Beluga Whale Committee (AIBWC) to make progress illustrates some of the difficulties that might be expected. In the case of the AIBWC, changing management goals and principles, unilaterally declared by one nation's government without consulting with the other partner to the agreement, doomed the initiative to failure.

In order to fulfill the instruction given the ICC Executive Council through Resolution 92-17, it was decided that a discussion document would be produced for the 1995 ICC General Assembly. This document was to be informative, to be useful for any further deliberations on the subject of Inuit whaling management that might occur. The report would, among other tasks, examine a number of management options, and would base suggestions for possible further action on the current realities existing in each country. Consequently, it was decided that in addition to community members' views, Inuit and non-Inuit decision-makers and leaders should be asked their views on a number of management-related questions. The interim report (entitled *The Inuit Whaling Agenda: A Choice for Inuit to Make*) was tabled at the 1995 General Assembly.

THE ENVIRONMENTALLY FRIENDLY NATURE OF COMMUNITY-BASED WHALING

We don't want to cause any evil to whales, we want them to remain forever.
Leonid Kytylin, Yanrakynnot, February 1995

As mentioned earlier, the notion that all whaling should cease, in order to prevent species extinction and to maintain marine-ecosystem integrity and biodiversity, is a common but erroneous belief. Understood superficially, such a notion might appear credible to many people. However, it fails to take into account the dynamic nature of marine ecosystems, the limited scale of current

FIGURE 31. Beluga hunting from a decked trap boat. Southampton Island, Canada, July 1961.

and planned whaling, and the high level of commitment whale users and managers have, today, for whale conservation and sustainable use.

Opponents of whaling rarely consider the environmental costs of replacing whale meat in the diet of whale-using peoples, or those few communities that might choose to return to using whale products as an item of diet. Although whaling contributes little to food production in global terms, it does help to reduce pollution of the land and sea that results from chemically intensive modern agricultural practices. For coastal peoples who continue to depend on local or distant marine resources, whaling helps reduce the pressure on commercial fish populations that would have to sustain an additional level of fishing pressure if there were no whaling.

It appears that environmental organizations and governments that work to oppose whaling seldom consider the possibility that environmental benefits can result from using whales for human food. In environmental terms, the costs of land-based agriculture are high, and include the loss of wildlife habitat and the associated reduction in biodiversity, soil erosion, contamination of groundwater reserves, heavy use of fossil fuels, release of various greenhouse gases, and a variety of drugs, hormones, herbicides, and pesticides being added to the environment and to human food supplies.

Whaling, in contrast, does not require any such chemical additives, nor does it contribute to loss of habitat, soil erosion, or groundwater contamination. Moreover, being an insignificant component of national and international trade, the marketing of edible whale products should not create the serious international tensions that are commonly associated with competition and trade wars caused by the heavily subsidized agricultural sectors of developed nations.

Whaling is also an exemplary food production technique, in comparison with other marine food-production systems. Few, if any, net fisheries are wholly selective in what they catch, and the same can be said about most fishing methods using hooks or traps. The coincidental by-catch and "waste" of nontarget, nonfood species may be quite high in many food fisheries, and these nonselective catching practices may result in the overexploitation of many nontarget species, including species or populations that may be in need of varying degrees of protection.

It is against this ongoing threat to (and actual reduction in) marine biodiversity that one can contrast the environmental benefits of highly selective and sustainable whaling. In whale hunting, a whale can be selected by species, by size, and (sometimes) by sex, before being taken; such selective hunting can reduce the threat to the reproductively active component of the population. It is this positive feature of whaling that allows Inuit to state with conviction that for centuries they have been, and continue to be, resource stewards and caretakers of animals.

THE BENEFITS OF INVOLVEMENT

A significant degree of indigenous control must be a governing principle in conservation management principles and sustainability strategies. It should enter strategic thinking: from initial questions of rights to land and subsistence base, through modes of collaborative and participatory research . . . to the issue of controlling interaction with the market economy.

IUCN Inter-Commission Task Force on Indigenous Peoples, 1997

It is now generally recognized by many international and government conservation agencies that the meaningful involvement of the resource-using community is essential if conservation goals are to be attained and sustained in a cost-effective manner. For resource use to be sustainable, it also has to be equitable. Sharing resources has never been a problem for Inuit or other indigenous peoples, but it does appear to be a problem for many who embrace an urban-based protectionist ideology and would see "owning" the right to decide that only nonconsumptive uses of animal resources is permissible.

This increasing involvement of Inuit whalers in whaling management appears to be occurring across the Inuit region, and, significantly, it occurs (for the most part) outside the context of the IWC. In Russia, Yup'iit have not, in the past, been included in the national delegation to the IWC, despite having asked for several years to be so involved. However, Chukotkan hunters are now working with Alaskans, together with Russian and American scientists, in connection with trans–Bering Strait beluga and bowhead studies. Perhaps such cooperation in the areas of research and monitoring may in time lead to a closer working relationship between hunters and managers—for hunters in the past were rarely consulted, since their knowledge was not recognized as being useful. Andrei Ankalin, an outstanding marine hunter at Sireniki, who has worked with scientists from the Russian Academy of Sciences, commented: *"scientists and hunters should study animals together. . . . It is good that [scientists] respect our knowledge, and we can tell you such facts that science does not know."* His views are echoed by Tatyana Achirgina, Vice President of ICC–Chukotka, who observed:

Clearly the knowledge of hunters is in some ways more detailed, and more profound and deeper than the knowledge of scientists, but it is used to a small extent, or not used at all. . . . [We] will work with the Russian Government and whaling organizations in other countries. I am convinced that numerous issues of whaling and whale conservation for future generations can only be resolved by joint efforts . . . Only a merging of knowledge, experience, and efforts of hunters and scientists can provide insight into the biology of whales, their conservation, and their improved traditional utilization.

In Alaska, the Alaska Eskimo Whaling Commission has developed excellent whaler-to-biologist/scientist cooperative arrangements, and the same cooperation may develop with respect to the Alaska Beluga Whale Committee (ABWC).

In the western Canadian Arctic, the Canada–Inuvialuit Fisheries Joint Management Committee manages bowhead and beluga hunting under comanagement agreements that have functioned well, with hunters working closely with scientists on joint research programmes and monitoring all beluga catches throughout the region. Further east, where comanagement structures have been more recently introduced, the intent is to ensure that communities are fully involved in decision-making, research, and monitoring, as they affect whaling activities.

The Canada–Greenland Joint Commission on Narwhal and Beluga involves representatives of the user communities in both countries as co-commissioners (together with a representative of each nation's responsible government department), and in all Canadian and Greenlandic whale management instances, Inuit traditional ecological knowledge (TEK) is considered in making decisions, alongside the knowledge provided by biologists.

In the Greenland case, the Home Rule authorities consult with Greenland national and community hunter and municipal organizations, and delegate a high degree of autonomy to individuals at the community level with regard to deciding local regulations that impact conservation actions taken by local hunters.

THE REGIONAL APPROACH
TO RESOURCE MANAGEMENT

Whales do not belong to anyone, but we should all think of them together.
Timofei Panangye, Sireniki, February 1995

As one moves to a greater degree of international regulation, so the user community becomes markedly, and understandably, less involved. This is so with both NAMMCO (the North Atlantic Marine Mammal Commission) and the IWC, where a decidedly "top-down" or state-management system operates. In the case of NAMMCO, the question is of less practical concern, for this newer organization has yet to play an active management or regulatory role with respect to whaling. At the present time, NAMMCO's principal concerns appear to be to provide scientific advice to an incipient management body, which at some future time may decide to assume management responsibility over several North Atlantic marine-mammal populations. However, it remains unclear when, or indeed whether, the NAMMCO state-management model will evolve into a more equitable power-sharing arrangement with resource-using communities. It seems most improbable that the IWC top-down management system will change in the foreseeable future. The majority position at IWC (which is the position that rules) reflects a western, urban-based animal-protectionist ideology; a western science–based influence is only apparent when it supports the majority's predetermined political position. The larger problem for whalers in the IWC context, then, is a lack of understanding and respect shown toward diverse cultures and a marked antipathy to whaling-community concerns. Such tendencies strongly suggest that the IWC is most unlikely to recognize any meaningful role for the user communities or to take advantage of their knowledge when making management decisions.

With respect to adopting a more regional approach toward resource use and conservation issues, it is noteworthy that several international environmental or resource-use organizations have adopted a regional approach toward northern issues. Such regional organizations include the Arctic Environmental Protection Strategy (AEPS), established by the eight Arctic Rim nations. These same eight nations—Russia, the United States, Canada, Denmark/Greenland, Iceland, Norway, Sweden, and Finland—have recently created the Arctic Council, which is meant to enhance conservation, sustainable use, and trade involving northern resources. The Northern Forum is a political association of regional governments from among the countries of the circumpolar north, while the World Conservation Union (IUCN) has also recognized the circumpolar north as one of its nineteen world regions for fostering and administering its activities. Each of these groups has a "sustainable use of living resources" programme, as do the International Arctic Science Committee and the UNESCO–Man and the Biosphere Programme (which has the circumpolar Northern Science Network as one of the regional MAB subprogrammes).

Within the circumpolar north, there exists one particular, and effective, regional resource-management regime that has operated for a quarter of a century: this is the international treaty that regulates the conservation (that is, sustainable use) of polar bears. In many ways this treaty contrasts markedly with the global reach of the IWC, though it does resemble, in certain respects, the more regionally focused NAMMCO. Membership in the polar bear regime is restricted to the five states within whose territories polar bears are found (Canada, Denmark/Greenland, Norway, Russia, and the United States). Although nations where Inuit hunt polar bears may or may not include community representatives on their delegations to management meetings, nevertheless, at a national level a high degree of user involvement, and hence accountability, occurs in managing polar-bear hunting and habitat protection in three of the four countries where Inuit hunt (these being Russia, the United States, Canada, and Denmark/Greenland). Polar bear management decisions are western science–based, but much of the actual research on polar bears involves the knowledge and active involvement of hunters whose expertise is based on extensive indigenous knowledge of bear behaviour and ecology.

In comparison with the IWC, the polar-bear management regime is quite small: five nations and no nongovernmental organization (NGO) observers participating in the polar-bear management regime, compared to thirty or more nations and around ninety NGO observers at the IWC. The nations involved with polar-bear management are restricted to the five range states, while the IWC membership is open to every nation. Thus, at present, there are two land-locked countries participating in the IWC and a majority of member nations who have never whaled nor conducted any significant management-relevant whale research.

This contrast between the membership characteristics of these two resource-management regimes highlights the question of equity in respect to decision-making. In the case of the polar bear regime, each member nation has a management programme supported by long-term monitoring and research activities; each member of the regime thus has a well-informed, and one might say validly "earned," basis for voicing opinions about shared management of the world's entire population of (noncaptive) polar bears.

In contrast, the IWC nations have potentially equal decision-making powers, yet they contribute in quite different degrees to the work of the commission. The fee structure ensures that the few whaling countries contribute far more financial and research resources than do nonwhaling countries. Many member countries neither conduct management-related whale research nor participate in the work of the Scientific Committee; in some cases, they do not even involve themselves in any of the technical working groups or subcommittees. Even with such minimal involvement (or such extensive *non*involvement!), these countries are able to consistently out-vote the interests and needs of the whaling nations. The imbalances that exist in this multination whaling regime make it virtually impossible for the minority whaling nations to have their whaling-treaty rights honoured, no matter how legal, scientifically justified, and treaty-consistent their requests happen to be. Under the present membership (and influential NGO) arrangements, an ideologically united voting bloc can—and in substantive terms, may often choose to—out-vote the minority and in the process subvert both the goals and the procedures set down in the treaty.

In view of the above, and remembering that whales also occur in geographically defined populations (so-called management stocks), it does appear that a regional approach might be a more equitable and cost-effective—and hence rational—way to regulate whaling. The extent to which such a more regionally based management system will produce equitable outcomes will also increase the likelihood that both resource use and the management regime itself are sustainable. The future of the IWC remains uncertain, as one commissioner or another in virtually every year reminds fellow commissioners; as the Chairman of the IWC recently stated:

> Now, in 1997, we have reached a stage where it is clear that some whale populations are recovering and a lot of progress has been made on developing the Revised Management Scheme (RMS) to control future whaling. Nevertheless, the IWC is at an impasse. Despite the moratorium, the IWC does not now control or regulate all whaling in the world . . . [and] such whaling has increased. . . . There are major differences of opinion within IWC. . . . The Irish delegation has become increasingly concerned that the inability of the IWC to reach consensus on fundamental questions concerning the RMS and other issues will lead to a breakup of the IWC. . . .

Indeed, with most whaling in the world taking place entirely outside the International Whaling Commission (*less than 5 percent of whales annually taken are under IWC control*) and IWC attempting to severely restrict or close down what little whaling it does regulate, the regime appears to be hastening its own demise by increasing its irrelevance in whaling matters. As one delegate at the 1995 ICC General Assembly noted when the whaling issue was discussed:

> . . . the ship of IWC is losing its ability to navigate. Its compass is influenced by incomparable [contradictory] forces, and it is navigating in foul waters. I expect it to hit a solid rock in the relatively near future. No one knows if it will be seaworthy again.
>
> *Ingmar Egede, speaking in Nome, Alaska, July 1995*

A ROLE FOR ICC IN THE REGULATION OF WHALING

> . . . it would be real nice if the ICC had a whaling commission . . . but these things take millions [of dollars] to do. My view is, if you're going to do it, do it right. . . . I would say, focus on the things where people need the most help.
>
> *Tom Albert, Barrow, April 1995*

Indeed, the resources required to initiate and maintain a functioning and credible ICC whaling management commission are a sufficient barrier in themselves. In addition, the Inuit from one member nation of ICC would almost certainly be prevented by their national government from associating with any such whaling organization, for such association would likely be construed as weakening the effectiveness of the IWC.

In each of the four ICC countries (Russia, the United States, Canada, and Greenland) Inuit whalers, working through community, regional, and national organizations, relate in various ways to their national governments with respect to whaling issues. In some of the ICC member countries, the Inuit and their national governments enjoy a good working relationship, or they are working at this time to improve the existing relationship. In such circumstances, given the different national statutes, management structures, and practices involved, the opportunity to create a four-nation ICC whaling body with management responsibilities is not feasible today. In practical terms, it seems prudent that Inuit in each country should, at this time, seek to create the best working relationship with their respective national government's whaling management authority.

At an international level, Inuit from two countries relate to IWC and NAMMCO either through national delegations or as observers. ICC is already an observer at IWC meetings, and it participates in other international fora where whaling issues of importance to Inuit are being discussed (for example, at CITES [Convention on International Trade in Endangered Species of Wild Fauna and Flora], and at the World Conservation Union [IUCN] and various United Nations meetings). The new Arctic Council (to which Canada, Denmark/Greenland, Russia, and the United States belong) is a forum where resource-use issues, including trade, are likely to be central topics for discussion. The ICC, as a Permanent Member of the Arctic Council, will have the opportunity to ensure that Inuit views on the whaling issue are adequately represented, should any national delegation fail to properly represent Inuit interests during relevant deliberations.

A number of areas of concern are shared by Inuit in each country; one such concern is for an adequate international defence of whalers' rights and needs. The question of an adequate education and communication programme to ensure that animal protectionists' views are debated and answered, both in the media and at international meetings, is another area where ICC might assist community-based whalers. In this regard, and mindful of the costs involved with taking such initiatives, ICC might seek to work closely with other organizations that have made communications and education a priority. One such international organization is the High North Alliance (HNA, representing the whalers and sealers of Greenland, the Faroe Islands, Iceland, and Norway, plus the Canadian Sealers' Association). The High North Alliance operates a Web site (*http://www.highnorth.no*), maintains a reference library, conducts an active programme working with journalists and other media persons, sponsors international conferences and panel discussions, and publishes a periodic newsletter (*The International Harpoon,* obtained from HNA, Box 123, N-8390 Reine, Norway).

The newly formed World Council of Whalers (WCW, an organization *"supporting communities engaged in sustainable whaling,"* P.O. Box 291, Brentwood Bay, B.C., Canada, V8M 1R3) will maintain a close working relationship with the High North Alliance so as to avoid duplication and to extend the HNA programmes globally. Among WCW committees will be an Education Committee, working closely with teachers, and expert committees dealing with human rights, legal affairs, and nutrition and health. The World Council of Whalers is a global, rather than regional, organization whose members' common concerns ensure a unity that likely overshadows geographical and cultural particularities. Whalers, representatives of whaling and whale-consuming communities, and whaling-nation governments from eighteen countries, provinces, and states—including Alaska, Canada, Chukotka, and Greenland—participated in the 1998 WCW General Assembly.

The programmes and resources available through the High North Alliance and the World Council of Whalers appear most relevant to the concerns of Inuit whalers, especially those related to maintaining Inuit cultural integrity, social well-being, and health.

CONCLUDING COMMENTS: THE INUIT WHALING AGENDA

> You are asking me about whaling and I am telling you about it. . . . It is nice to even speak about whales, and whaling is the main joy in our lives. . . . The time of whaling is the best time of life. You respect yourself, and you respect nature. . . . The whale unites hunters and their families, takes away from our life all the minor things, all the garbage. When we are hunting, we become better individuals.
>
> *Petr Typykhkak, Sireniki, February 1996*

Whaling today is carried out to fulfill the nutritional, social, cultural, economic, and other essential needs of small-scale coastal communities. Whaling persists in regions of the world where land-based food production is seriously constrained by geography and climate. In such locations, people wishing to produce food for their own families, or to make a living providing food for others, are making a rational choice by engaging in the taking of whales from the seas. In such coastal societies, edible whale products often constitute traditionally valued staples in the community's food culture.

The proclaimed "environmental" justification for any international ban imposed on sustainable whaling is not supported by objective, ecological evidence. And the environmental costs of providing nutritionally equivalent land-based or marine-derived substitutes for whale meat and mattak are, in comparative terms, extremely high. At the same time, the sustainable use of whales by Inuit and other small-scale coastal whaling communities appears, in conservation terms, to be entirely beneficial.

The notion that "use is bad," that all whales everywhere require total protection, is a recent ideology advanced by urban-based animal protectionists. However, though emotionally appealing to some people, such an ideology flourishes in the absence of objective knowledge about whales, whaling, and the whaling peoples whose lives continue to be enriched by their own multiple

FIGURE 32. A single fin whale contributes a significant quantity of economical and nutritious fresh food to many families. Kangaatsiaq municipality, Greenland, October 1989.

interactions with whales and other cetaceans. In addition, sustainable whaling can also be viewed as an environmentally friendly food-producing activity. In the larger view, the sustainable use of living, renewable resources holds the key to humankind's long-term survival on this planet. Subjecting Inuit's, and other coastal peoples', customary whaling practices to relentless attacks that infringe on their rights under international law is ignorant, unwarranted, perverse, and socially destructive:

> It is difficult for me to explain what the bowhead means to us, the Sireniki people . . . When hunting was banned it seemed that our soul was killed. I don't know how we are going to live. . . . If the bowhead whale continues to be hunted, we shall remain; otherwise we shall be lost. . . . If there is no hunt, we shall go quickly, one after another. My brother Yukah was the first to go— and now he is calling me. . . . We are deprived of half our life without them.
> *Andrei Ankalin, Sireniki, 1993*

The goal of this book is to place current concerns that Inuit have expressed about the future security of their whaling activities into an appropriate cultural, institutional, and moral context. The initial reaction to mounting threats posed to whaling by a variety of nonlocal agencies was to consider establishing an ICC body to assume greater management responsibility and control. Even if such an institutional response is not practical at the present time, a more realistic response for the ICC may be to ensure that Inuit in all four member nations are fully aware of recent international, as well as national, developments related to Inuit societies' shared interrelationships to whales and whaling. Thus, the role of such a so-called Inuit Whaling Agenda will be to keep Inuit organizations and whalers informed of actual or proposed changes taking place in whaling management. This book is a beginning contribution to make such information more generally available, even as it provides a framework for assessing future developments that may take place.

There appears to be a need to maintain Inuit unity on the whaling issue. The strategy adopted by those who would oppose whaling is to divide whalers into different groups: thus, Inuit are presently in one group (the so-called aboriginal-subsistence whalers), separated from other community-based whalers hunting similar species by similar means elsewhere. Diversity among Inuit whalers is displayed in two important characteristics. The first relates to the degree of involvement of Inuit in monetized trade in whale products, with Greenland and Chukotka whalers including market practices in their everyday economic transactions, Canadian Inuit being allowed by national law to engage in such practices if they so choose, and Alaskan Inuit effectively being denied that right. One other dimension of diversity also separates the Alaskan whalers from the other three countries' whalers—namely, their ability to expend considerable sums of money to justify their continued whaling.

Inuit might consider whether any advantage would follow from a more unified response to various external demands, which tend to divide the Inuit whalers into those who can afford the huge amount of time and money to undertake research and monitoring (for instance, the Alaskan bowhead hunters) and those (that is, all the other Inuit whalers) who cannot expend such vast sums of money on an annual basis to research as thoroughly (in a western science framework) the whale populations on which they depend. When considering this particular issue, it is important to know that these ongoing financial demands may bear no relationship to the need for information to satisfy management requirements. The demands for more and more research expenditures, in the context of the International Whaling Commission, appear to be the strategy adopted by people opposed to whaling who seek to harass and punish whalers through the imposition of heavy financial requirements, in their efforts to protect whales from being hunted.

The various actions being taken to oppose sustainable whaling, if continued or successful, not only threaten Inuit and other whaling peoples' social security—by diminishing or destroying these societies' cultural capital, they also represent a potential loss for all humankind. People around the world are increasingly aware that indigenous and local communities that maintain traditional relationships with their environment through the sustainable use of local resources have much to teach those who have lost those living connections to the natural world. Indeed, the loss of a specialized cultural adaptation from the progressively reduced inventory of sustainable food-producing activities cannot be considered to be in the best long-term adaptive interests of the global community. The future problems of providing food for an expanding human population, and of ensuring social justice and environmental quality under conditions of growing uncertainty and demand, are among the greatest challenges that face international resource management agencies today—and in the future as well.

Under such circumstances, the lack of environmental leadership and objective analysis displayed in the international whaling debate, together with the ethnocentrism and intolerance for cultural diversity that are everywhere to be found, are not only regrettable, but in environmental and human terms, dangerously irresponsible.

Inuit and Whales

This account of Inuit whaling opened with a statement by a Chukotkan whaler, Nikolai Gal'gaugye: *"There are many wonderful animals, but whales are best of all. As they pass by . . . you immediately come to understand your place on the Earth, and you become warm inside. . . ."*

Throughout the pages of this book, the historic and continuing importance of whales to the Inuit—for a variety of different reasons—has been described. These varied reasons often appear utilitarian and practical: whales as sources of food, health, economy, or whales as means to maintain social relationships, culture, and spiritual beliefs.

Nikolai Gal'gaugye's words, though, indicate that there are other reasons for valuing whales. Indeed, whales have an intrinsic value, an ability to inspire wonder and good feelings. Nor is there any inherent contradiction in valuing an animal for important practical or utilitarian reasons while at the same time appreciating it for aesthetic or emotional reasons, as this statement from a student in the eastern Canadian Arctic indicates:

> Whales are such beautiful and intelligent creatures. They appear so carefree as they swim in our waters. They have always been in the lives of Inuit—as respected animals and traditional food.
>
> *Allan Nakoolak, Sakku School, Coral Harbour, March 1995*

This sense of value, of respect, whether or not the animals are taken and used, results in a concern for whales that is apparent in the statements of Inuit from all regions of the Arctic that have appeared earlier in this book. For example, these comments by Chukotkan hunters:

Whales do not belong to anyone; we should all think of them together. . . .
Whales give us quietness and beauty of life. . . . We don't want to cause any
evil to whales—we want them to remain forever.

Such statements reflect a personal connection that many feel toward
whales; Jamie Kataluk wrote from Sakku School, Coral Harbour: *"whales are
important to me in a personal way, because they are nice to watch when they are
swimming."* Yup'iit hunters, in Chukotka, also speak in personal terms: *"I
always think of the bowhead whale—I always watch them playing—I am becoming a whale myself. . . . It is nice to even speak about whales—[and] to respect
him—you understand that you are the same as they are, and they are the same as
you. . . ."*

These statements make it clear that to Inuit, as to people elsewhere, whales
are special. Inuit, through their involvement in international efforts to safe-
guard the arctic environment and to engage in whale research, monitoring, and
management, have indicated that arctic whales are their responsibility, and that
they will continue to exercise stewardship in regard to these magnificent creatures. This stewardship manifests itself through working with researchers and
government agencies in the Arctic and in diverse international fora, as well as
through spiritual safeguards effected by prayer and traditional rituals.

For such determined conservation measures to continue, the culture and
personal commitment of Inuit whale guardians must remain strong. For non-
Inuit, the need to understand how their own actions help, or hinder, this front-
line conservation effort must be seriously considered.

Inuit Communities Mentioned in Text (approximate population)

Aklavik: Mackenzie Delta, Inuvialuit Settlement Region (500 Inuvialuit)

Anadyr: Chukotka Regional Centre (10000; 60 Yup'iit)

Anaktuvuk Pass: Brookes Range, inland from North Slope (300)

Arctic Bay: North Baffin Island, Nunavut (450)

Arviat: West Hudson Bay, Nunavut (900)

Aasiaat: West Greenland (3600)

Avan: Chukotka; community closed in 1941

Avanersuaq: North Greenland municipality (900)

Barrow: Alaska North Slope (2300)

New Chaplino: Chukotka (320 Yup'iit; 90 Chukchi)

Clyde River: Northwest Baffin Island, Nunavut (350)

Coral Harbour: Southampton Is, NW Hudson Bay, Nunavut (500)

Enmelen: Chukotka (30 Yup'iit; 320 Chukchi)

Gjoa Haven: King William Is, Central Nunavut (700)

Grise Fiord: Ellesmere Island, Nunavut (100)

Hall Beach: North of Hudson Bay, Nunavut (300)

Igloolik: North of Hudson Bay, Nunavut (800)

Ilulissat: West Greenland (4700)

Imtuk: Chukotka; community closed in 1932

Inuvik: Mackenzie Delta, Regional Centre (3200)

Ittoqqortoormiut: East Greenland (600)

Kangaatsiaq: West Greenland (1700)

Kivak: Chukotka; community closed in 1952

Kivalina: Northwest Alaska (350)

Kugluktuk: [Formerly: Coppermine] Nunavut (800)

Lake Harbour: South Baffin Is, Nunavut (300)

Lorino: Chukotka, (70 Yup'iit; 1050 Chukchi)

Lyon Inlet: NW Hudson Bay, Nunavut (seasonal use)

Maniitsoq: West Greenland (4200)

Naukan: Chukotka; community closed in 1958

Nunligran: Chukotka (25 Yup'iit; 320 Chukchi)

Nuuk: West Greenland, Capital city (13500)

Nuiqsut: Alaska North Slope (350)

Pangnirtung: East Baffin Island, Nunavut (1200)

Point Hope: Northwest Alaska (600)

Pond Inlet: North Baffin Island, Nunavut (1100)

Provideniya: Chukotka [Regional centre (5500) 125 Yup'iit]

Qaanaaq: Northwest Greenland (650)

Rankin Inlet: West Hudson Bay, Nunavut (1750)

Resolute: Cornwallis Is, Nunavut (180)

Saint Lawrence Is.: Bering Sea, Alaskan Yup'iit (1000)

Sanikiluaq: Belcher Is, SW Hudson Bay, Nunavut (450)

Shingle Point: Yukon North Slope, seasonal settlement site

Sireniki: Chukotka (310 Yup'iit; 210 Chukchi)

Tuktoyaktuk: Inuvialuit Settlement Region (800)

Upernavik: West Greenland (2900)

Uummannaq: West Greenland (2800)

Wales: Alaska Bering Strait region (150)

Yanrakynnot: Chukotka (30 Yup'iit; 320 Chukchi)

APPENDIX B

Glossary

ABWC: Alaska Beluga Whale Committee

AEWC: Alaska Eskimo Whaling Commission

Agenda 21: 1992 U.N. international environmental agreement

AIBWC: Alaska-Inuvialuit Beluga Whale Committee

baidara: Chukotkan native skin-covered boat

CITES: Convention on International Trade in Endangered Species of Plants and Animals

DFO: Department of Fisheries and Oceans [Canada]

ESA: Endangered Species Act [U.S.]

FJMC: Fisheries Joint Management Committee

HCH: Hexachlorocyclohexane [toxic man-made chemical]

floe-edge: Edge of sea ice that extends unbroken from shore

ICC: Inuit Circumpolar Conference

ICRW: International Convention for the Regulation of Whaling

IFAW: International Fund for Animal Welfare

Inuit Tapirisat of Canada: Canadian national Inuit organization

Inuvialuit: Inuit occupying the western Canadian Arctic

Inuvialuit Settlement Region: Inuvialuit homeland in the western Canadian Arctic

Iñupiat: Inuit occupying North Alaska (singular: Inupiaq)

KNAPK: Greenland Hunters and Fishers Organization

mattak: The skin and portion of underlying fat of whales—a highly valued customary food of all Inuit throughout the North—Greenlandic spelling; elsewhere, variously maataq [beluga mattak], maktak [Canada, N. Alaska], mangak or mantak [Alaskan and Siberian Yupik], mataq [bowhead mattak], muktuk [anglicized spelling]

MMPA: Marine Mammal Protection Act [U.S.]

MOU: Memorandum of Understanding (agreement between parties)

NAMMCO: North Atlantic Marine Mammal Commission

NOAA: National Oceanic and Atmospheric Administration [U.S.]

NSB: North Slope Borough [Alaska]

Nunavik: Inuit homeland in Northern Quebec [Ungava]

Nunavut: Inuit homeland in Eastern and Central regions of the Northwest Territories [Canada]

NWMB: Nunavut Wildlife Management Board

PCB: Polychlorinated biphenyls [toxic man-made chemicals]

PCC: Polychlorinated camphene [toxaphene, a toxic chemical]

PBR: Potential Biological Removal

sassat: A winter opening in the sea ice containing trapped whales (other spellings: saussat, savssat)

SWG: Scientific Working Group

TEK: Traditional ecological [or environmental] knowledge

umiat: Alaskan skin-covered boats (singular: umiaq)

U.N.: United Nations

UNCED: United Nations' Conference on Environment and Development [in Rio de Janeiro, 1992]

UNCLOS: United Nations' Convention on the Law of the Sea

WCED: World Commission on Environment and Development

Yup'iit: Inuit occupying Siberia, islands in the Bering Sea, and western Alaska; also spelled Yuit (singular: Yupik)

Index

The following typographical conventions are used in this index: *i* and *t* denote illustrations and tables, respectively.